ACCESS TO SCHOLARLY INFORMATION

LIBRARY MANAGEMENT SERIES

ACCESS TO SCHOLARLY INFORMATION:

ISSUES & STRATEGIES

edited by

Sul H. Lee

Dean, University Libraries
Professor of Bibliography
The University of Oklahoma

THE PIERIAN PRESS
1985

Library of Congress Catalog Card Number 85-60595
ISBN 0-87650-189-7

THE PIERIAN PRESS
P.O. Box 1808
Ann Arbor, MI. 48106

For Melissa

Contents

Introduction

Providing access to scholarly information has increasingly become an important challenge for academic libraries in recent years as economic difficulties have forced librarians to seek more innovative ways to meet users' needs. The demand of scholars for information has steadily increased though access to resources has become more difficult. Libraries, for instance, have turned to resource sharing in the form of bibliographic networks and consortia to respond in part to the new challenge of information delivery. In addition to budgetary difficulties, other recent developments also have affected the ability of research libraries to meet the needs of scholars: rapid developments in computers and telecommunications; copyright law revisions; increased demand for information in nontraditional formats; and advancements in preservation of library materials.

The issues of access to scholarly information are enormously complex. Librarians, scholars and publishers need to work together to find some solutions. An attempt is made in this book to look at, from the librarians' perspective, several important dimensions of the problem. They include the definition of access and how it is perceived by faculty and librarians. Also considered is the design of library buildings and the arrangement of collections in terms of providing improved physical access. Other questions considered are the conflict between preservation and access, new developments in reference such as online access, and collection building to enhance access to scholarly information. Technical service also impacts access and issues such as automation and AACR2 are presented. The effects of copyright legislation on photocopying, reserve books, and fair use are discussed, as are technological developments which will speed up and enhance access to scholarly information. In summary, the papers address how research libraries deal with problems of access to information in the 1980's.

Contributors to this volume are 1) Herbert S. White (Dean, School of Library & Information Science, Indiana University), "Ownership is Not Always Availability--Borrowing May Not Satisfy

Access Needs"; 2) David Kaser (Professor, Library & Information Science, Indiana University), "The Role of the Building in the Delivery of Library Service"; 3) Kenneth G. Peterson (Dean, University Library, Southern Illinois University), "Challenge or Dilemma: The Impact of Collection Development, Reference Services, and Preservation on Access to Library Resources"; 4) Helen H. Spalding (Head of Technical Services, University of Missouri – Kansas City Libraries), "Recent Developments in Technical Services and Their Implications for Access to Scholarly Information"; 5) Carolyn Bucknall (Assistant Director for Collection Development, General Libraries, University of Texas--Austin), "Conjuring in the Academic Library: The Illusion of Access"; 6) Donald E. Riggs University Librarian, Arizona State University), "Reduction in Rights and Access"; 7) Robin Downes (Director, University Library, University of Houston), "Electronic Publishing and the Scholar's Workshop"; 8) Robert A. Seal (Director of Library Public Services, University of Oklahoma Libraries), "Issues in Access to Scholarly Information: A Bibliography."

I would like to express my appreciation to Mrs. Pat Webb for her assistance in the preparation of this volume and to Mr. Donald C. Hudson and Mr. Robert A. Seal for editorial assistance.

Sul H. Lee
Norman, Oklahoma
December 1984

Ownership is Not Always Availability –
Borrowing May Not Satisfy Access Needs

Herbert S. White

I am pleased to contribute a paper to this volume dealing with access to scholarly information, with an emphasis on the word access. I make this point at the very outset because most of our preoccupation as a profession, and particularly in academic libraries, has been with the evaluation and measurement of libraries through their ownership and holdings. Access not very many years ago meant the ability to find an item in the library's card catalog. If that location was successful, then the library's role in providing access had been successfully fulfilled. Whether or not the item could be retrieved for the individual requestor within 30 minutes, one hour, one day, two days, or one week, was a secondary and perhaps irrelevant question which had nothing to do with the values of the library. If the material was already charged out, that was hardly our fault. Lest the reader think that my statement is a gross exaggeration I would note that to this day, few if any libraries have any statistics concerning their ability to respond to the need for items in their own collections. If the material is in the catalog, what percentage of it is available immediately? What percentage within two hours, one day, one week? It has been stated that half of the material in the catalog is not on the shelf on the day it is requested, but to my knowledge we don't have hard core informa- tion, or really any way of getting it. It would require us to imple- ment a policy under which we somehow got individuals who looked for a book and didn't find it to report that to us. Right now, many of them simply take another book (whether or not it is as good we will never know nor will they), or leave the library, and say nothing to us.

Concern with collection rather than access is of course the faculty view. Faculty are not as concerned with access questions. Much of what they need they have already pre–empted away to their own offices, so that in this case ownership equals access. Ownership concerns also get in the way of fostering interlibrary cooperative activities, and will continue to as long as we are counting volumes. My response at a cocktail party to the question "Why don't academic libraries cooperate more in their acquisitions pro-- grams?", was "libraries are likely to cooperate more when the presi- dent of the university stops having cocktail parties to celebrate the x millionth acquisition." I almost ended up with a drink dropped on my foot.

Access as differentiated from ownership is of course a major concern for secondary users, but many of these are students, and library policies are rarely made for the benefit and with the input of student concerns. Trueswell postulated his 80–20 rule as long ago as an article in the *Wilson Library Bulletin* in 1969.[1] Most simply, his rule is an expression of the Bradford distribution curve. 80% of document needs can be satisfied from 20% of the collection. Of course, the Pittsburgh study by Galvin and Kent[2] said the same thing, and I found it fascinating that at least some of the criticism came from individuals who didn't really attack the methodology or conclusions, but stated the premise that such a study should never have been done, because it played into the hands of the ene-- mies of libraries. I consider that nonsense.

That ownership and access can present contradictory value systems during times of budgetary stress (such as for the last 10 years, now, and for the foreseeable future) becomes clear in the results of an Indiana University National Science Foundation funded study[3] on which I reported in an Oklahoma University sponsored conference several years ago. We found that as budget cuts required decisions on what *not* to buy, the most immediate candidates were duplicate copies and duplicate subscriptions. Not necessarily because they weren't being used -- they presumably were -- but because from the standpoint of holdings these duplicates were "frills" which didn't count. Over a period of only about five years, the duplication rate of periodical subscriptions in academic libraries fell from 5% (a figure I would already consider suspiciously and unnaturally low given the number of branch collections) to less than 2%. It is only after we have cancelled these "frill" duplicates that we are prepared to tackle the question of what we might have that nobody is using, or is unlikely to use. Those predictions are not hard to make. As Kent and Galvin noted, material not used in the first year or the first five years is not likely to be used in the next hundred years, either. Yes, the possibility exists, but the probability does not, and collection decisions should at least be based on an estimate of reasonable probability, unless you are prepared to acquire every- thing. Not even the Library of Congress does that.

It is clear that the academic library materials budget is aimed at ownership and not at access. Perhaps the most blatant example is the practice of charging users for the cost of interlibrary loan,

2

but not charging them the cost of a book they have appropriated as soon as it was cataloged and have kept in their office for the last ten years. Charging for interlibrary loan represents, for me, a logical absurdity in any case. It amounts to a double penalization for the user. The first comes from the fact that you didn't buy what I am now asking you for. I am sensible enough to recognize that you can't buy everything, but I could probably make a case that this acquisition would have been more reasonable than some of the things you did buy. However, I won't even do that, because I realize that second guessing is unfair. I am therefore willing to forgive you for not already owning what I have just requested. However, your insistence in now penalizing me twice — first from the standpoint of time because I have to wait and secondly by attempting to charge me — stretches all credulity, and I refuse to play along.

I realize, of course, why academic libraries have so much difficulty in paying for so-called peripheral activities such as on-line searching and interlibrary loan. They are peripheral only because they weren't anticipated, at least not in the budget. Most library budgets I have seen spend about 2/3 of their money on staff salaries, and of course that is never enough, certainly in our view. Most of the remaining third goes for material purchase, and of course that is never enough, for either the librarians or the faculty. The materials budget will certainly never be adequate no matter what it is. Nothing or virtually nothing is held back for contingencies or unexpected expenses. This then is why we can't pay for on-line searches. Not because they are more expensive than manual searches. Perhaps they are and perhaps they aren't. The point is that the budget may not have anticipated any such costs, or at least certainly not enough.

An emphasis on collection subverts an emphasis on access because of the continuing competition for funds. As noted in our NSF study, it simply is not contest. It also means that in looking for access alternatives we are looking for the cheapest and not necessarily the best way, or ways to stick the user with the cost of anything we didn't buy. The emphasis on holdings count as a measurement of value goes back to days when there was plenty of money and the strategy worked. Both faculty and library administrators were first and foremost collection builders — incidentally if at all managers or with a service orientation. The statement "we will be remembered not for the service we gave but for the collection we left behind us," which some of you may recognize and identify, correctly characterizes the period. At the present time, when many academic libraries are indeed being run by qualified and competent administrators capable of making alternative value judgements,

3

we find that the faculty is still playing the old game by the old rules.

We should recognize very quickly that when faculty (and you will already see that I identify faculty as the major obstacle to progress and change) talk about the quality of the library, they are really talking about quality stated as the size of their part of the collection. To faculty the library is a balkanized organization, and they watch to make sure they get what they perceive as their fair share of the acquisitions pie. There is really no way for us to deal with this problem except ultimately directly and in a straight-forward manner. The size of their collection piece becomes part of their own security blanket, and part of the mechanism by which they seek and achieve recognition and approbation from their own colleagues in the same field in other universities. The problem reaches its critical and most tragic point when we have a faculty member who stubbornly insists that the library develop a collection expertise in an area totally outside the university mission, because it is an area in which he or she *wishes* the university were active. Faculty, who can be useful in ranking two books or two journals in their own field to see which is better, but not in deciding that both should be bought (they must work within finite guidelines) don't in all honesty know anything about what makes a good library. This is why concerns of access haven't really permeated faculty bodies. There is really no reason faculty should know very much about this – I don't know what makes a good cyclotron or a well structured fugue, either. But who is going to tell them?

The proper and, obviously at this stage, idealistic answer to the question asked so often from outside but also inside the field -- how many books and journals do you have? – is I really don't know and I don't care. Does it matter? What is it that you need to know? The exercise works for me at least in principle, although I recognize there might be more difficulty in applying it in practice. I have asked faculty colleagues "If I promised to deliver to your office within 72 hours any book or journal article you have requested, would you care where I get it from?" Their answer is always that they wouldn't care. Actually, 72 hours probably provides me a margin of safety, because I am quite convinced that even present technology would comfortably permit it in 48 hours or even 24.

If we are to extricate access as a significant priority, we need access budgets, and we need them as a broader substitute for the far more specific materials purchase budgets. By far the greatest portion of the expenditure will still go for purchase, but some for interlibrary loan costs, some to bibliographic access, some to copy-right royalty payments, some to photocopying, some to payments for commercial services, some for the development of even faster, more accurate and higher quality delivery mechanisms. It is after all part and parcel of the same problem.

Satellite accessibility for the transmittal of text has been available for some time, and individuals in Hawaii long ago stopped relying on airplanes to bring them films of football games. I served in 1975 as a member of the consultant team for what was to be the new Pahlavi National Library in Iran. The library never happened, for reasons I am sure you understand. However, the report still exists at least in fragmented volumes, it could be reconstructed, and it has some value even nine years later. We planned interlibrary loan from the British Museum and the Library of Congress to Teheran via satellite, with local delivery via helicopter because the roads were not good enough. That was 9 years ago, and it was not then nor is it now a far-flung technological breakthrough. All of the technology was available then, and it is old technology now. We don't need to be nearly as esoteric or expensive, but we do need to do a great deal more than we are doing, if we are serious about doing for the access problem what we have done for the collection problem.

In our attempts to develop systems for access beyond ownership, we immediately turn to "funny money" solutions such as interlibrary loan. They are funny money approaches in part because we don't really want to know what it costs to lend -- certainly not in the true economic sense of burdened expense categories. The best we will do is identify out of pocket expenses, and we do even that reluctantly. Interlibrary loan is still justified as a cooperative activity, and buttressed by the insistence that it provides a mutual benefit for all of us. There is even the suggestion that it involves a moral or higher duty to the profession. Of course, we know that services provided as a favor are furnished at the convenience or pleasure of the provider, and will usually take a low priority when compared to other and more important functions. I find this sad, because it has burdened us with an antiquated and archaic mechanism, which stands out particularly in contrast to the rapid strides we have made in developing bibliographic access systems. Alternatives are available, but they cost more. What is saddest of all is the fact that users have accepted this value system and these delays as reasonable. Users are not critical of library services, and almost any survey of user reactions to the local library will produce a favorable response -- except perhaps with regard to materials purchase. We pay dearly for this lack of critical expectations, although it does make things easier for us. Please allow me to give you three specific examples from my own observation and background.

I do a fair amount of industrial library and information center consulting, much of it oriented to an evaluation of present library services. Even though hardly anyone ever complains, sometimes the librarians and sometimes upper management know there are problems which should be addressed. As part of this process I try to schedule interviews with a random sample of professionals in the organization, some heavy library users, some non–users or very peripheral users. All are high in their praise of the library, and all blame themselves for any lack of further use of the facilities. Ultimately, the one service virtually all of them use is interlibrary loan. I ask them how the service works and they say it works fine. I ask them how long it takes to get a response and they tell me it varies, usually from a few days to several weeks and sometimes more than a month. I then ask them if they think that is reasonable. I invariably have to repeat the question because they don't understand it. They believe it is reasonable as a delay because we have told them it is reasonable, and of course that is nonsense. For some users a lengthy delay causes no problems, for others it makes the entire process irrelevant. We have no real way to adapt to the specific situation and to change our procedures to suit. We might if the client is willing to pay more, and we will happily let him use his own resources to satisfy his request.

I know a faculty member at another university who once shared a particular problem with me. He is a full professor, a graduate of an Ivy League institution, and not easily intimidated -- except by library policy. Confronted by the need to verify a reference from a work he planned to use for a class assignment, he proceeded confidently to the library catalog and located the call number of the item in question. There was no copy on the shelf, and his inquiry at the circulation desk produced the information that there were two copies, one lost and one charged out. It might return any time but was not due for two weeks. Defeated, because he needed the material by Friday, he returned to his office and deleted the reference from his reading list.

Why? Why did he accept an inventory report instead of a plan to furnish him with the needed material? If the library's copy is out, or lost, or at the bindery, and the need for a copy by Friday is realistic, is it really true as assumed that the interlibrary process could not meet the request in time? Of course not, if we are prepared to deal with individual need rather than with organizational procedure. A rapid contact of the OCLC file will indicate quickly if the material is included in the collections of one of the neighboring state universities, located less than 200 miles away. A telephone call will determine whether the material is on the shelf, with the request that it be charged out on interlibrary loan and left at the main circulation desk. The paper work, if indeed there must be

6

multi–carbon paperwork, can follow. A further call to the university travel office will identify at least a half dozen faculty members on the neighboring campus, planning to return (probably by car) within the next 24 or 48 hours. Would they be willing to pick up the material, as a favor to a faculty colleague if not the library? Of course they would. Why don't we ask them? Because it never occurs to us. It also never occurs to us that offering a status report, or an explanation of why the item is not available, is neither a solution nor an answer.

A doctoral student at Indiana University is currently completing a dissertation under my direction. In it, he compares and contrasts the interlibrary loan practices of chemistry librarians in industry and chemistry librarians in universities. There are substantial dif–ferences, and they are largely attitudinal. Some of them involve a greater expenditure of funds, but not all. Industrial librarians of course never charge their users for the cost of interlibrary loan. They recognize, or at least someone does, that such a practice would be pointless because ultimately the cost would still be borne from parent organizational funds. Of course, the same thing is also true in universities, because I doubt that very many faculty members pay the interlibrary loan cost from their own personal pockets. At least, not in the universities with which I am familiar.

There are other differences. Industrial chemistry librarians are free to use their ingenuity and interpersonal contacts to obtain needed material as quickly as possible. Many requests are made over the telephone. Academic libraries, which usually have a greater access to terminal equipment, rarely use it for this purpose. Most academic chemistry branch heads are not even allowed to make their own requests, but must rather submit the request to a central interlibrary loan office. That function, which has no direct contact with the original requestor, places the request through its own procedures, and either mails the material to or contacts the re–questor. The branch librarian doesn't even know when or whether the request was filled.

Industrial chemistry libraries report that they make heavier use of commercial services during peak load periods or when the interlibrary loan clerks are backlogged. In academic libraries the user just waits longer, because the process doesn't change. Of course that costs more, but why don't we budget for it?

For librarians to face issues of access we have to separate them from issues of ownership, because ownership is only one form of access. Even ownership does not guarantee access – not if some–body else has the material first. As a teaching faculty member who both adapts library procedures to my own needs and my own strategies to procedures I can't change, I note with some assurance

7

that the reason that individuals such as myself don't return things to the library is in part because of a value system which makes books in our offices (even if we didn't buy them) appear impressive. It is also because if we have any expectation of needing material again it is safer to hang on to it. I don't return it because I don't trust it to be there if and when I want it again, and of course that becomes a self--fulfilling prophecy. I trust the library's purchasing system a lot more than I trust its access system.

Once we begin to look at all aspects of access as alternative solutions to one and the same problem, we can perhaps begin to dismantle the present antiquated and obsolete system of interlibrary loan which has choked off response quality for so long, and substi-- tute for it a system which validates itself on economic grounds. That is, economic ground for the librarian, because that individual now has the choice between purchase and a more temporary or request--driven form of acquisition. Richard de Gennaro,[4] in his talk at Indiana University's own copyright seminar in 1977, was not making that point directly, but it emerged at least peripherally. The copyright borrowing limitations for a particular periodical title posed no problems for him, and as far as he could see should pose none for other academic libraries. Anything borrowed so fre-- quently as to approach the CONTU guidelines should be bought, because it is certainly being used more frequently than much of the material which is being bought. De Gennaro is correct, in his appeal to reason. I would feel better if I could buttress that point with an appeal to the pocketbook. What should be the crossover point economically where repeated borrowing is more expensive for the borrowing library? We need such an economic motivator because the motivator of anticipating the user's requests by having more copies of fewer things obviously does not persuade us. And, of course, if librarians pay for purchase but individuals pay for borrowing we have destroyed the ability to compare.

Interlibrary loan will work well when it is economically driven to motivate the supplier, as of course it now does with commercial services. That should also apply to academic lenders, who should be encouraged to charge not only out of pocket cost, but all direct cost, burdened with overhead as in any proper accounting system. In fact, if we can provide a little extra beyond that, we might even get lenders to compete in service quality and speed for the privilege of lending. Will it cost more? Of course it will cost the borrowing library or whoever is subsidizing it more, although the money will presumably stay within the larger system, and those libraries which both lend and borrow will break even. Lend is an outmoded term when applied to the periodical articles which comprise most of scholarly transactions, anyway. Articles are not lent, photocopies

8

are sent for retention.

To the extent to which the acquiring library can successfully seek subsidies for this process, I wish it good luck. Those subsidies can perhaps be furnished by the parent institution, perhaps by the state, perhaps the federal government, perhaps some benevolent foundation. The options are as open as they are for the support of other library activities. However, to charge the user for this transaction when he is not charged for the books the library has bought for him to keep in his office, and when the need to acquire from the outside really results from your decisions and not his, is illogical and unfair.

What is the cost of supplying material at a proper reimbursement rate? Commercial services provide something of a clue of bottom cost, because it certainly costs the supplying academic library, bureaucratically structured as it is, more than that. Perhaps $10 on the average, perhaps as much as $15. We really can't control that figure, or at least shouldn't try, to any greater extent than to which we influence the cost of books and periodicals we purchase. The relationship between the economics of purchase or of other forms of access can then be easily established, and we can even establish a cut–over point between purchase and each–time–we–need it acquisition for every title. Obviously, there is a cost involved in all of this and we don't have enough money. But then, we never have had enough money, don't have it now, and won't have it in the future. But we have failed to accept the fact that other costs of access (bibliographic as well as document) are as legitimate a kind of library cost as the purchase of material which will sit on the shelf and, at least according to Trueswell, Kent, and Galvin, be used by nobody. Our attempts to diffuse or minimize the cost of interlibrary access leads us into all sort of nonsensical ground rules designed to even up the burden of lending, precisely because it is still a burden. Requesting libraries are supposed to go through a geographically based system of priorities in deciding from whom to request material. The doctoral dissertation to which I referred earlier found that industrial special libraries, perhaps because they are more pragmatically driven, ignore that injunction. I could have told the student that, too. When I was an aerospace industrial special librarian in Texas in the late 1950s we acquired almost all of my interlibrary loans from Georgia Tech. Why? Because they had almost everything I wanted, because they were accurate, and because they were fast. If someone had demanded I first try the Texas Engineers Library I would have responded that I used to try the Texas Engineers Library first, and that was why I now requested from Georgia Tech.

Georgia Tech never complained, and never asked why they

had been singled out for an attention level which sometimes ex--ceeded 25 requests/week. They never charged me, either, and perhaps that was wrong. If they had charged me, I would have had to make my case to my own management for budgeting this cost, and perhaps this would have allowed me to make a stronger case for a larger purchase budget. As management then saw it, and perhaps in many libraries still does, the difference between purchase and other forms of access was between a cost and no cost, and that made decisions easy. Too easy.

Although I have been addressing this issue in more general library terms, and drawing some of my examples from the special library sector, I believe that it applies just as well to research libraries and the use of scholarly materials. We have known for some time, or at least should have known, that the acquisitions emphasis dif--ference in scholarly libraries comes largely from what librarians and faculty members historically perceive, and not from what they do. They want large inclusive collections because of the security and prestige which this brings to them and their academic depart--ment, not necessarily for the way the material will be used. We have known for some time that scientific research as funded by federal agencies (and these are the source of funds for most scientific research projects) tends to be applied research. There is very little basic research carried out in universities, and where it is, it still does not start out with an exhaustive literature review, except for doctoral students who carry no real clout. It starts with a pre--mise, with a hypothesis, with a paradigm, and then seeks evidence to support the conclusion already reached. Evidence which refutes or clouds it is definitely not welcome. As social science research became more and more heavily dependent on government priorities and wishes in the 1950s, 1960s and 1970s, the same description applied here as well. However, there is now at least some evidence that even humanities research may not in all cases be as massively collection--oriented as we have assumed. A member of our NSF study advisory committee, a distinguished professor of theology, stated with confidence that virtually any doctoral program in theol--ogy could be supported from a collection of 2000 books, and that in fact he had already identified those books and seen to it that they were moved from the main library to the Theology Department.

Questions of whether or not we provide adequate access services are in any case a matter of concern primarily to us librarians, because for our users alternatives to the library increasingly exist. These include alternatives in bibliographic access, available on a terminal to anyone with an electric outlet and a few dollars. They also include alternatives in document delivery services, available increas--ingly as an output option of the bibliographic process, and available

10

via telephone line, telefax, or one day delivery service. How often do most libraries use Federal Express or Purolator to acquire infor-mation? How often is UPS used to ship material?

Access, both bibliographic and document, can increasingly be done by just about anyone. It only costs money. And, yet, at the same time, I consider it suicidal for libraries to attempt to pass off this process directly to their users, or to users urged to work directly with other information intermediaries. This is some-thing some academic libraries have begun to do increasingly with regard to on–line searching for the silly and correctable reason that it costs money and staff time. In neither case does the refusal to take on this responsibility result in cost reduction for the institution, it only shifts the cost and the responsibility, and as I have already noted in other writings it is a very unwise ceding of library responsi-bility, or library turf. We certainly don't understand turf as street gangs understand it. It is unwise for us to ignore this concern because control over the bibliographic and document access process is only the preamble to the much larger and much more important struggle we must fight and we must win if we expect to retain our signifi-cance in a technologically shifting information era. That struggle will concern the role of librarians as information intermediaries and information interpreters, and it is that struggle we must under-take as soon as we put access concerns behind us.

REFERENCES

1. Trueswell, Richard W. *Some Behavioral Patterns of Library Users: The 80/20 Rule.* Wilson Library Bulletin 44:458–461, Jan. 1969.

2. Kent, Allen, and others. *Use of Library Materials; the University of Pittsburgh Study.* New York, M. Dekker, 1979.

3. White, Herbert S. *Publishers, Libraries, and Costs of Journal Subscriptions in Times of Funding Retrenchment.* Library Quarterly 46: 359–77, Oct. 1977.

4. De Gennaro, Richard. *The Major Research Library and the New Copyright Act.* p. 147–162 of The Copyright Dilemma, edited by Herbert S. White. Chicago, American Library Associa-tion, 1978.

The Role of the Building
In the Delivery of Library Service

David Kaser

We talk much in the library profession about the importance of effective techniques for the delivery of library services but, except for occasional pre–conferences on buildings, we seldom discuss the role of architecture itself upon the quality of library service. That will be the purpose of this paper. I intend to discuss here the importance of careful planning in the distribution of functions and of the rational layout of furniture and equipment throughout library buildings in facilitating access by scholars to documents, information, and staff services.

The role of the library building may be discussed at three levels of sophistication:

1) as simple shelter;

2) as abetting library function;

3) as enhancing esthetics.

These three levels moreover are given here in a descending order of necessity. The building's role as shelter is imperative; it *must* keep our books in out of the wind and weather. Its role as abetting library function is a desideratum; it *should* enable us better to deliver a desired quality of library service. And its role as enhancing esthetics is permissive; it *can* make for us a more beautiful experience than we will otherwise have.

This paper will concentrate on the second level of sophistication given above – as abetting library function. There is not much that we librarians can do about the first level anyway. If the roof leaks or the building falls down, it is seldom if ever the librarian's fault. Although I will not discuss the third level, I hope no one believes that I am against beauty. If architects can also supply beauty without jeopardizing the building's first two obligations listed above, so much the better, but it *must* be subordinated to them. Scholars

13

should seek out libraries because they meet their purposeful ends effectively; if they want a sensuous, esthetic experience, they can visit the Grand Canyon, or a fine restaurant, or turn on the stereo.

Functional Layout

Entries. A library building's role in abetting the delivery of library services begins at the front door. The style and design of the doors themselves can contribute to the ease with which the building can be used. Doors that twist on swivels rather than swing on hinges can impede entry into a building rather than facilitate it. Single–leaf doors distribute traffic evenly across a range of portals, whereas double–leaf doors create traffic congestion where the two leaves meet. In North America, and in most other parts of the world, traffic has a natural tendency to bear to the right; thus entry doors, when differentiated from exits, should constitute the right wing of portals.

This relationship of entry to exit doors, of course, is often dictated by the configuration of services immediately inside the building, but that configuration should in turn be mandated by the logical flow of library functional activities rather than result simply from happenstance. If a patron is going to need staff assistance, for example, that need is most likely to occur immediately upon entry rather than later. Experienced reference librarians moreover have stated that if they can see the eyes of a patron walking in the door they can tell whether or not help is going to be needed. These two facts largely dictate a location for the reference desk just inside the main door and on its right. The circulation desk, on the other hand, is usually the last place patrons stop to check out books before exiting the building. Thus its logical location is to the left of the entry (or right of the exit), if crisscrossing traffic in the lobby is to be kept minimal.

These would seem to be very simple and rational considerations, yet how many libraries have you seen where they have not been observed, where entries and exits are reversed? Calculate the vast number of people who, over the half–century life of the building, will waste ten or fifteen seconds trying to come in the "out" door, or will unnecessarily jostle each other in the lobby, jarring loose books and pencils, and stepping back and apologizing. How many reference desks have you seen clear across the lobby from the entry, or tucked behind the elevator, or in another room, forcing information–seekers to ask preliminary questions about their location before they can ask the questions to which they really need answers. Similarly rational determinants should also govern the locations of other library functions: public catalogs, periodicals, media

14

services, etc.

Signage. Much, of course, can be accomplished through the use of a good system of directional signs. Historically libraries have been notoriously poor in their use of signs, although our time--honored reluctance to use signs seems recently to be breaking down. Good architects are trained and skilled at providing systems of graphics that can lead people through complex structures to their intended destinations, no matter how remote. To realize how effective architects can be at this task, one need only consider how easy it is for travellers to circumnavigate the globe, and traverse innumerable airports, where languages (even writing systems) differ at every stop, without once having to stop and ask a directional question. It is not unrealistic to aspire that no library patron should ever have to ask a directional question. We must, however, tell architects that we need and want signage systems if we are to expect them to be provided.

It is worth noting in this connection that we librarians could aid greatly in this effort to help patrons find their way through our buildings if we took the time to ponder what our terminology means to others than ourselves. We have expropriated a number of good words out of the English language for our sole use with little thought given to how this use might misguide rather than aid the patron. A sign reading "Documents" is no help to a patron who has assumed that everything a library purveys is a "document." "Reference" to many means a footnote; "circulation" is what happens to one's blood; a "catalog" (misspelled, of course) is a book (or "document") issued annually by Sears & Roebuck. One must admire the stark functionalism of the sign above what amongst ourselves we librarians would call a reference desk but which instead reads simply "Get Help Here," or of the stack designation "Big Books" instead of the more frequent and cryptic word "Folio."

We are also unhelpful when we use initialisms that mean little to others. "HRAF", "OCLC", "SuDoc Nos.", "LC", or "PC" come to mind. Designating decentralized libraries by their subject content rather than by the fortuitous name of the donor of the building would also help in way--finding. "Agriculture", "Chemis--try", or "Rare" mean more to most people than "Mann", or "Swain", or "Spencer." Indeed it sometimes seems that if we were more concerned with deskilling library use through such con--siderations as these, we would not have to spend so much time teaching library skills in our BI programs.

Distributing Furniture and Equipment

Seating. Access to library services can often be improved by devoting greater attention not only to the rational layout of library functions throughout a building but also to the logical distribution of furniture and equipment within a department or area. For pedagogical, structural, and library professional reasons, we began about a century ago to separate books into closed stacks and patrons into public reading rooms rather than allowing them any longer to cohabit the same space, which had been the practice earlier. From about 1880 until after World War II virtually all library buildings were constructed in this mode, and as our institutions grew so did our reading rooms. Monumental reading halls, such as those at the New York Public Library, or at the University of California, or at Columbia, or at Michigan, came to be regarded almost as status symbols; bigger was better, and we vied with other for superiority in the amount of acreage we devoted to reading tables.

Regrettably we never asked readers in those days if there were other configurations of reader stations that they might have preferred. Even if we had asked, however, we would unlikely have found much new, because by the very building designs that we had over the decades imposed upon them we had led patrons over time to assume that reading in a library was synonymous with reading in a large reading room. We had offered them no options to select from. It was not until after the Second World War that the advent of modular building design concepts permitted us once again to mix books and readers throughout our library buildings in any ratios that we (or they) may have wished. Research into reader preferences for study space began in the 1950s and 1960s, and we began to learn that our patrons much preferred to study either in privacy or in small "human--sized" areas rather than in the big reading rooms that had for so long been our pride and glory.

The diffusion and adoption of the results of those investigations have taken an unfortunately long time. Architects, senior faculty and academic administrators, and often even we librarians, still think and talk of "reading rooms", as though they are something that every self--respecting library should have, whereas they are really obsolete. Patrons prefer seating either in privacy, as in perimeter carrels, or in semi--social settings comprising a few varied reading accommodations, perhaps between eight and twenty--four diverse reader stations, scattered in various locations throughout the building in proximity to the materials that they intend to use. Thus an admixture of stacks and seating clusters is the configuration preferred by our patrons.

Stacks. There are some useful principles to bear in mind, however, as we come to lay out this admixture of stacks and reader stations. A first principle is that we should make patrons go through

16

stacks to get to reader stations rather than run them through reading areas to get to stacks. This is not, as is sometimes suggested, in the vain hope that the freshman who came to the library to study his French 101 may, en route to a seat, take off the shelf and read a copy of Plato's *Republic*. It is rather that a patron seeking a library book is very likely to disturb readers unnecessarily if he must traverse a cluster of seats to get to the shelf.

Stacks, when located between readers and major traffic ways such as aisles or stair–lobbies, can do much to mitigate the potential distractions of sound and activity. Books on shelves are excellent sound–absorbers and constitute very serviceable acoustical treatment for an area. Regrettably, however, designers and architects tend to consider loaded bookstacks less attractive than reader accommo-- dations, especially lounge seats, and as a result they usually propose to locate seating in the most visible and congested parts of the building rather in its farthest reaches where it serves its purposes better. How often have you seen clusters of lounge furniture located right where the elevator debouches its passengers, to the distraction of anyone trying to study there? We librarians should be alert to, and understanding of, this tendency and take pains to reverse it wherever we see it.

A second principle to be observed in laying out an admixture of stack and reader space is that, come what may, the integrity of the classification system as the library's book--finding mechanism must be preserved if access to materials is to be facilitated. No pockets of book–stack should be tucked away beyond clusters of reader stations or hidden behind restrooms or stairwells. Ideally, as one steps off the elevator, the range–labels for all of the stacks on the floor should be arrayed sequentially before him, so that no time need be spent in unproductive reconnaissance before the desired book comes to hand. Again one has only to multiply the time spent on this single search by the hundreds of thousands of similar searches that will be made during the lifetime of the building to see how critically important this matter is. If an efficient stack layout can result in saving five seconds per book fetched, that over fifty years is a great gain in human economy.

One additional principle to be kept in mind in distributing reader accommodations throughout stack areas is that the distance from any shelf to the nearest seat should never be allowed to exceed a certain reasonable maximum. Perhaps thirty feet is the maximum that a patron should have to carry a book off the shelf before finding a seat of some kind. Of course we can never assure that the seat will be empty when it is needed, or indeed that the patron will even opt to use the nearest seat, but patron efficiency and library function will be enhanced if the travel time required from shelf to seat is kept low. Incidentally such a layout also keeps down the distance, and therefore also the time and energy, required for a staff member to return a book to the shelf after it has been found on a table.

An Ambience for Study

It has long been the case that engineering factors have caused more dissatisfaction with library buildings than have considerations of any other kind. Librarians can conceptualize functional work-- flows and distributions of activities that are efficient for both them-- selves and their patrons, and architects can design buildings that incorporate these program requirements into structures that are both technically sound and esthetically pleasing. But it has often happened that these functional and beautiful buildings have been plagued by problems of poor lighting, inadequate air treatment, or bad acoustics, all three of which are really engineering matters. Regardless of who is to blame for these deficiencies, however, any one of them can destroy the building's environment for study and impair its ability to render good library service.

Lighting. One would expect that, considering all of the research that has been done into illumination, it would by now be a simple matter to light a library building for best study conditions, but such is not the case. If it were left up to us librarians to determine, we would resolve it immediately, but also unidimensionally, based upon the needs of our patrons. We know from our experience that library patrons are best served when we provide them a uniform illumination level (usually in the range of 50–60 foot--candles at table–top height) of high quality, fluorescent light throughout the entire building, except perhaps in such areas as restrooms and stair-- wells that will be forever dedicated to the non--study functions for which they were originally intended.

Regrettably, however, three other conflicting pressures are often brought to bear upon lighting decisions in libraries that can, and frequently do, muddle what should be a simple issue. These three pressures result from esthetics, from economics, and from market forces. Some designers feel that uniform illumination throughout large spaces is ugly, dehumanizing, and institutional, appropriate perhaps for supermarkets but out of place in libraries. They prefer to perceive lighting as part of the interior design poten-- tial of the library, as an area of concern that should be subject to their esthetic attention in the same way as fabrics, colors, finishes, and furnishings. Lighting, in this view, should be crafted and shaped as part of the interior landscape. Obviously it is not their intention to make study more difficult as a result of this motivation, but

18

it does nonetheless happen in too many cases that their desire to project contrasts of light and shadow, or to hide light sources, or to introduce a variation of designer fixtures (often table-- rather than ceiling--mounted) results in areas and spaces that are inade-- quately illuminated to be effectively used for reading. Thus some library interiors in recent years have been lighted more appropriately for such multipurpose spaces as hotel lobbies, bistros, lounges, and clubs than for libraries which have only a single reason for being, namely for research and study.

A second consideration that has been brought to bear in recent years upon lighting standards in libraries is one of economics. Until ten years ago power was relatively cheap, and institutions worried little about their electric bills. When power prices shot upward in the middle of the last decade, however, many institutions carried their economizing too far and cut too deeply into the amount of illumination allowed to library study. Given simplistic instruc-- tions, usually in the name of patriotism, to cut power consumption by twenty--five per cent, many colleges and universities simply sent crews through all campus buildings pulling every fourth tube out of light fixtures, regardless of whether or not the intended purpose of the space could still be fulfilled. No doubt some libraries had previously been overlit, but it is also a fact that many libraries still suffer from this mechanistic and irrational approach to energy conservation.

The same motivation has also led in the past few years to over-- reliance upon windows for lighting in libraries. Natural light is very fickle illumination and cannot be relied upon for reading in libraries. In the first place, daylight prevails through only half the hours that most libraries are open, and in the second place great shifts take place from moment to moment in the amount of illumination provided by that daylight. Direct sun, of course, is impossible to read by, and even indirect natural light causes disintegration of book paper, but nonetheless many libraries con-- structed in the last ten years have been carelessly fenestrated to the east, west, and south. The recent introduction of light--sensitive supplemental sources of artificial illumination and of effective ultra-- violet filters in window glass, however, suggest that we may at last be on the way to solving some of the most nagging and chronic economic problems of library lighting.

Market forces have also sometimes worked to the detriment of good library lighting. This is a large and dynamic industry, where sales pressures have been known to result in overlighting of library spaces. The virtues of task--lighting have in many cases been oversold, even in academic libraries where task--lights are severely subject to vandalism and theft, requiring frequent repair or replacement. Given our present grasp of the multitudinous issues involved in library lighting, it seems that we librarians should still strive to obtain the uniform ambient light levels for our patrons that we have long recognized as being best for their purposes.

Heating, Ventilating, and Air--Conditioning. Another engineering matter that can seriously affect a library's ability to facilitate use of its materials is the manner in which it is heated, ventilated, and air--conditioned. Many library buildings that are otherwise very successful find their service capability impaired by deficiencies in this important area. Inside air is either too hot or too cold, or too damp or too dry, or temperature and humidity are not uniform-- ly distributed, or there is inadequate turn--over of air either in the entire building or in certain of its zones.

Such environmental deficiencies as these harm library activities in a number of important ways. Perhaps of greatest immediate significance is that patrons are discomforted by them and are unable to make full use of our study facilities. Staff are likewise troubled and rendered less efficient by such conditions. Extended departures moreover from the middle ranges of temperature and humidity (say 68 to 76 degrees Fahrenheit and 45 to 55 percent humidity) have long been known to have a debilitating impact upon the life expectancy of book paper, causing preservation problems in our collections. The introduction to computer hardware into libraries has brought with it its own set of even more rigorous heat and humidity tolerances that must be observed if systems are to function properly and reliably.

Perhaps a principal cause of inadequacies in library heating, ventilating, and air--conditioning is poor communication among all of the parties who should be involved in their planning. Engi-- neers must know where heat is likely to build up, so they need to be cognizant of the architect's intentions regarding the locations and sizes of windows as well as the kind of glass that will be used. They need also to be apprised of the plan for lighting the building, where and how many cool fluorescent tubes will be used and where hot incandescent lamps (if any) will be installed. They need to know the intended functions of the different spaces in the building so that they can accommodate the heat--generating differentials of such areas as computer rooms, or concentrated study areas, or general stacks. They must be made aware of where, if anywhere, cigarette smoking will be allowed so that they can duct those spaces more fully than other areas. In addition, however, the owner must be informed as to the trade--offs involved in cutting cost in the installation of environmental control features. Too often well engineered systems are subverted by ill--advised decisions made by the institution, usually in last--minute haste, to attempt to econo--

mize on controls. Good environment controls are not cheap, but they are of great importance to the effectiveness of library operation and service, and they are therefore a poor place to look for economy in construction cost.

Acoustics. Sound levels taken by themselves have little relevance to the success or failure of an ambience for study. Relatively high background or continuous sound seldom distracts from concentration; in fact, it is often used intentionally to mask over the kinds of sounds that do distract. These tend to be such occasional and unexpected, obtrusive, interruptive noises as individual voices or footfalls (as contrasted with a blended hum of many such sounds), squeaking wheels on booktrucks, honking horns, slamming doors, or poor typists (as contrasted with the rhythmic cadences of good typists). It is an ironic likelihood that more patrons are probably distracted by the shrill voices of librarians than by any other single factor.

By far the best acoustical treatment that has ever come to the aid of librarians desirous of developing a good study ambience is the installation of carpet on the floors. It does more to deaden and absorb sound than any other building material or device thus far invented. Regrettably, however, many library buildings have not yet taken full advantage of its availability. Too few libraries use carpet where it is needed most, namely in the lobby, presumably because harder materials last longer under its heavier traffic, but this is misplaced economy. Not only can the considerable din of entering and exiting patrons be ameliorated by carpet in the lobby, but also carpet here can quickly establish an appropriate inner tone for the library that contrasts with the hardsurface stone or concrete walkways of the building's exterior where louder noises are to be expected. Without carpet in the lobby, patrons simply keep on talking until they get even further into the building, disturbing readers wherever they go.

The use of carpet on the floor does not relieve library building planners of other responsibilities regarding acoustics. They must continue to use acoustical ceiling tile and to take acoustical consideration into account in the distribution of functions, equipment, and furniture. Wallhangings, or even carpeted walls, can aid in attaining a desirable sonic environment, and such acoustical devices as soundabsorbers are sometimes necessary as well. Properly used, the sounds of air moving through ducts, or of motors running, or even of bubbling fountains, can aid in covering over other distracting sounds.

The introduction in recent years of atria and open wells into building design is a major cause of sonic distraction to library patrons. Since there is nothing up there to absorb or baffle sound,

21

as chairs and stacks do on the horizontal plane, noise is transmitted unimpeded vertically through atria, disturbing patrons on whatever levels are reached by them. Design considerations moreover often call for these open wells to be located above busy lobbies which then, especially when uncarpeted, echo their hubbub sometimes all the way to the roof (or more frequently to a hard–finish sky-light), rendering the entire building unsatisfactory for study.

... And Flexibility

Also, in the last analysis, we enable ourselves to deliver best library service over the long future when we design and construct buildings that are flexible, buildings that can be easily and economi-cally modified through time as reader needs change. This need for flexibility has not always been recognized. Historically through-out the centuries, and indeed right up until after World War II, we built library spaces that we intended to use forever for the purposes for which they were originally conceived. But we are very conscious today of the rapid acceleration in the rate of change in all areas of human endeavor, including libraries. Given such awareness, it would seem to be the height (or depth) of hubris today to plan buildings that do not allow every opportunity for effective and economical alteration as reader needs and library capabilities continue to evolve.

Yet some architects do attempt to design, and some institutions do accept, library buildings that unnecessarily and expensively tie the hands of our professional progeny, buildings that have no chance ever of meeting future functional requirements that we are unable now to anticipate or foresee. These buildings are fated ignominiously to be razed before they get old, of being uncere-moniously knocked down before they fall down, simply because they are unable to adapt to any uses other than those for which they were originally planned. It is bad enough for many of us to have to contend with inflexible old buildings constructed before change had become so inexorable an element in our society or before modern construction methods became available to facilitate alteration. But it is well–nigh unforgivable to construct a new such building today.

What are some of the requisite features of a maximally flexible building constructed today? Obviously, and most often mentioned, is that they should have few if any load–bearing walls, that the entire weight of upper floors should be carried on columns so that partitions can be removed and relocated as needs change. Few library buildings constructed today violate this dictum, but flexi-bility is often severely impaired in a number of their equally egregious

22

ways.

The aforementioned use of atria and open walls handicaps future building adaptation. It is seldom practicable to floor over atria at upper levels, so the hole in the center of the building is likely to remain where it is as long as the building is in use, largely dictating a limited range of possible functions that can ever go on at its bottom. If ten years from now, in order to accommodate an unforseen new direction in campus growth, we relocate the library entrance in a new wing and wish to convert what is presently the lobby into office space, we are unable to do so, because no one wants an office with a ceiling sixty feet high.

Using anything other than a uniform pattern of ceiling light fixtures also limits future use of space in a library building. If, for example, the original installation used ceiling lights only in reading areas and relied on shelf--mounted fixtures in stack areas, the possibility of swapping these two locations later on is much reduced, no matter how imperative future circumstances would seem to make it. Any librarian with two years of experience knows how easily things can be moved if it requires only that they be picked up and moved, and how difficult it is if it also requires that a work order be submitted requiring workmen to come install a new system of ceiling lights. It just does not get done.

Understandably also uniform heating, ventilating, and air--conditioning treatment should also be sought throughout a building. And except in very special circumstances, such as a need to install compact shelving, a uniform floor--loading capability should be designed into the structure. A number of recently constructed libraries feature cantilevered areas which would be unable to carry the weight of stacks, even if good practice should dictate that they be relocated there. Uniform ceiling heights are also desirable throughout a library building to abet flexibility. Just as atria, mentioned above, limit the use of space, so do exceptionally low ceilings. When ceilings are dropped down to the top of 7' 6" stacks, for example, it diminishes greatly the future desirability of that space for reading or other library functions.

For almost two decades now far--sighted librarians have fretted about how to build into a structure the kind of flexibility we will ultimately need to accommodate a fully computerized but only vaguely delineated library service, with its elaborate power and telecommunications requirements. Complex (and expensive) grids of empty conduits and ducts have been built into slabs and well structures to enable us to bring cables throughout the building at some future time when we *may* need to operate terminal stations in locations presently unforeseen. This problem, at least, seems now to be on its way to resolution with the introduction of flat cables which can be strung anywhere, right on top of the floor slab, and then covered up with carpet–tile, giving even a higher level of flexibility than was made available with the more expensive conduit grids.

Although a number of new library buildings have recently been built with tightly constraining fixed–function elements, the need for flexibility is more often compromised in enlarged buildings rather than in buildings designed *de novo*. Usually the most func-- tional kind of enlargement to a library building adjoins it alongside an extended dimension, so that all library activities in the expanded structure can flow freely between the old and the new portions. Architects sometimes feel, however, that it is difficult to effect an attractive merger of old and new in this way, and as a result the new portion is often designed to stand as free as possible of the old building, with connection allowed only grudgingly through a kind of umbilical cord or nexus. This seldom works well, as library functions are infrequently adequately separable to permit their relegation to an adjacent structure without damaging the inherent unity of the work of the library. The reduction in flexi-- bility in the future use of library space when it is bifurcated in this way is obvious.

Conclusion

The nature of the physical facility that houses the library does indeed have a large, although somewhat unpresumptuous, role in determining the library's ability to deliver scholarly information. Too often we tend to view the building in which we do our work as a given, as an environmental constraint around which we must fashion our services, rather than as an integral part of our service itself, subject to our shaping and molding into accord with our patrons' greatest needs.

To be sure, once in place buildings can be very intractable, but given adequate attention in their planning to the rational layout of activities and furnishings, to the requirements of an appropriate ambience for study, and to flexibility, most could probably do better to support us in bringing service to patrons than they are presently doing. It behooves us to invest heavily of our time and creativity in making our buildings work for us rather than against us. They can be among our worst enemies, but they can also be among our most powerful allies if we will expend the effort to win them over to our side.

Challenge or Dilemma: The Impact of Collection Development, Reference Services, and Preservation on Access to Library Resources

Kenneth G. Peterson

Access to library collections and information sources has become a high priority for librarianship in recent years. Several examples illustrate this fact. Advertisements appeared recently for access librarian and head of access services positions at two major universities. In each case they listed responsibilities in areas such as circulation, interlibrary loan, document delivery, collection development, resource sharing, space planning, preservation, and library security. A news item in the *Library Journal* last summer reported the activities of a company in Albuquerque, New Mexico, called Access Innovations, Incorporated, which is in the business of providing online indexes for nonprint instructional media, including films, slides, filmstrips, videotapes, records, audio tapes, overhead transparencies and motion picture cartridges.[1]   Finally, in 1983, the American Library Association established the Commission on Freedom and Equality of Access to Information "to reexamine some basic tenets that determine how the American People gain access to information in order to function as productive members of society."[2]   An interim report of the commission was given during the recent ALA meeting in Dallas.

While not new in library usage, the word *access* appeared relatively infrequently in the literature of librarianship until quite recently. For instance, in checking the indexes to classic texts on library administration, such as *The University Library* (2nd edition, 1956) by Wilson and Tauber, *The Administration of the College Library* (3rd edition, 1961) by Guy R. Lyle, and *University Library Administration* (1971) by Rogers and Weber, we find hardly more than passing references to access–related activities like accessioning, new acquisitions, controls for special collections, and limitations on non–university readers. In scanning *Library Literature* it is mainly in the last half–dozen years that entries on the subject of *access* appear.

Changes that have occurred during the past decade related to collection development, reference services, and preservation of library materials have accounted in large measure for the increased interest in access to libraries and information sources. These changes stem from the proliferation of information in our society; the corresponding increase in production of books, journals and various non--print media as vehicles of communication; the use of computers to generate, store, retrieve and disseminate information; and the growing awareness that deterioration and decay threaten the life of large library collections. At the same time it is apparent that financial resources at most institutions are insufficient to deal with all these matters. As a result of shifts in collection development activities, changes in reference services, and greater concern for preservation needs, we are confronted with both challenges and dilemmas as we try to develop new patterns and chart new directions, while retaining what has been valuable in the past. This situation is summed up by Patricia Battin of Columbia University, who wrote, "Universities are now faced with the dual challenge: we must provide new structures of access to knowledge in an increasing variety of formats and, at the same time, continue to preserve, manage, and make available scholarly information in the traditional printed formats with appropriate links between all formats."[3]

Let us look more closely at each of these areas -- collection development, reference services, and preservation -- in terms of the challenges and dilemmas they present and their impact upon access to information and resources.

Collection Development

A distinguished collection, consisting of books, journals, microforms, maps, documents and materials in various other formats, is the heart of an academic or research library. Even though libraries have undergone many changes in recent decades, few librarians or library users could disagree with this view. Furthermore, as Dorothy Koenig of Berkeley reminds us, "The stated objective of the library regarding collections is to identify, acquire, organize, and disseminate all forms of recorded information which are pertinent to existing research and instructional programs."[4] While collection development has been a distinguishing aspect of library and archival work through the ages, during the twentieth century it has come to be recognized as a dynamic process involving the fine art of careful selection and evaluation. In the college or university setting, collection development must reflect the institution's mission and goals, the scope of its curriculum and levels of instruction, the research interests of graduate students and faculty, and the extent to which programs and services are offered beyond the

26

local campus. It is dependent upon the availability of resources for purchases; this, in turn, reflects the interest and commitment of campus administrators and members of governing boards.

In many institutions collection development policies exist in order to provide guidance and direction in the selection process. According to Y.T. Feng of Harvard, such policies "define the library's goals and objectives, identify the short–term and long–term needs of the community it serves, assess the degree of strength and weakness of its existing resources, and determine the depth and scope of its acquisition policy."[5] By means of policy statements clearer understanding is achieved in matters such as responsibility for making selection decisions, the forms of materials that will be collected, the levels of depth for collecting in various subject fields, the extent of collecting in foreign languages, and the local or regional users' needs to be met. As a means of checks and balances on collecting activities, libraries also need to evaluate their collections from time to time to measure their adequacy and quality, to consider whether they are satisfying users' needs, to identify and remedy deficiencies, to assess how well funds have been allocated, and to determine whether the library's and the institution's goals are being achieved.

Collection development, therefore, has a direct effect upon access to library and information resources because it determines first of all whether or not the collection contains the kinds of materials that are needed. The unfortunate but inevitable fact is that few if any libraries, including even those whose collections may range between five and ten million volumes, are able to cover all subject fields in all languages and with sufficient depth to meet every potential user's needs. The sheer volume of materials produced each year and the ever–growing rate of publishing, the restrictions imposed by budgetary limitations and the problems of inflation, and the dual concerns of housing and preserving collections preclude the self–sufficiency of any library.

Not new to our generation, this fact was realized by our predecessors who began exploring ways and developed programs in the hope of achieving combined collection strengths. One of the earliest examples of these efforts was the coordinated acquisitions agreement worked out between the libraries of the University of North Carolina and Duke University in 1931; and one of the more recent is that developed between the University of California at Berkeley and Stanford University in 1976. In both cases the agreements included not only cooperation in collection development, but also in granting reciprocal borrowing privileges for users and in direct lending between the participating institutions. Programs on a broader scale were also developed, such as the Farmington Plan begun in 1948 as a means for spreading among members of the Association for Research Libraries the responsibility for collecting foreign materials. In a related but different effort the Latin American Cooperative Acquisitions Program (LACAP) also operated during the fifties and sixties to assure that materials important for research from South and Central American countries were being acquired by libraries in the United States.

The interest of the federal government in cooperative collection development is reflected by the PL–480 program, which used dollar credits in foreign countries to acquire research library materials; and the National Program for Acquisitions and Cataloging (NPAC), initiated by the Library of Congress in 1972, as a successor to the Farmington Plan. The list of cooperative and joint efforts is extensive, but we would be remiss in not citing the significant role of the Center for Research Libraries, which was launched as the Midwest Inter–Library Center in 1949; the Universal Serials and Book Exchange in Washington, D.C.; the Center for Chinese Research Materials sponsored by ARL; and several agencies, such as MINITEX in Minnesota, WILS in Wisconsin, and ILLINET in Illinois, which exist to promote resource sharing primarily within their own states.

One of the most recent and exciting developments intended to improve access to resources is the Research Libraries Group's collection development Conspectus. According to Nancy E. Gwinn of the RLG staff, and Paul Mosher of Stanford, who were both involved in its design, "The Conspectus is an overview, or summary, of existing collection strengths and future collecting intensities of RLG members. Arranged by subject, class, or a combination of these, its divisions contain standardized codes that describe collection/collecting levels on a scale of 0 to 5 (with 5 as 'compre-- hensive')." Looking to the future its planners hope the Conspectus will become "the cornerstone of a larger national cooperative ef-- fort . . . among all the principal research libraries of the nation, for the eventual benefit of generations of scholars."[6]

According to Gwinn and Mosher, in designing the Conspectus the following objectives were agreed upon: (1) the need to identify collection strengths nationally, (2) mutual reliance and interdependence in providing research materials, (3) establishing a tool to identify collection levels at participating institutions, (4) the capacity to control physical growth of library collections and operating costs, and to distribute collecting responsibilities, (5) developing a mechanism to locate needed research materials more adequately, (6) rationalizing and standardizing the format and terminology for local collection development policies, (7) developing a mechanism to store or dispose of locally unneeded materials, (8) relating collection policies to preservation policies, and (9) relating collecting policy and responsibility to cataloging priorities, and establishing centers of cataloging. As a working tool the Conspectus consists of a matrix in which member libraries are listed along a horizontal axis and subject descriptors are placed on a vertical axis. Within the convergence of these lines collecting levels are indicated at any of six possible levels, including: 0 – out–of–scope, 1 – minimum level, 2 – basic information level, 3 – instructional support level, 4 – research level – and 5 – comprehensive level. The information provided by the Conspectus will enable librarians and scholars to know where major research collections in particular subject fields may be found. It will also help research libraries to discern patterns of strength and to plan collection growth without costly duplication.

An older and organizationally more structured plan to promote access is the ILLINET system in Illinois, which has been operating for the past twenty years and has recently been supplemented by the Illinois Library Computer System and the Intersystems Library Delivery Service. Established by action of the state legislature, ILLINET consists of eighteen Regional Library Systems, four Research and Reference Centers, and three Special Resource Centers. The Regional Library Systems provide primary back up collections to the public, school, academic and special libraries in their respective geographical areas. In addition to maintaining broadly based general collections, some areas of special collecting responsibility have been agreed upon in order to avoid duplication. The four Research and Reference Centers serve as back–up collections for the Systems by lending materials or providing copies of items to the Systems upon request. The four R and R Centers include the University of Illinois at Urbana–Champaign, Southern Illinois University at Carbondale, the Illinois State Library in Springfield, and the Chicago Public Library. The three Special Resource Centers – the University of Chicago, Northwestern University and the John Crerar libraries – may be called upon to provide items not found in one of the R and R Centers. About the mid–seventies, when the need for better bibliographical access was apparent, funds were provided to microfilm the card catalogs of the four R and R Centers and to distribute copies to each of the Systems.

Although mail service and TWX facilities were initially used by ILLINET to communicate requests among the Systems and R and R Centers, two computer–supported means of access have been developed. The first was the installation of CLSI circulation control and data bases at the State Library and six of the Systems located in the northern region of the state, with the ability of these libraries to access each others records. The second and more extensive has been the implementation of the Library Computer System (LCS) as a centralized statewide bibliographic data base and circula–

tion system. Although not used by the State Library or the Systems, LCS has been installed and is now operating in twenty–five academic libraries (including all thirteen state–supported universities), and LCS terminals have been installed at the State Library and all eighteen Systems in order to access the central data base. LCS, which supplements ILLINET, provides bibliographic access to 8.1 million titles and 13.2 million volumes in Illinois academic libraries; during 1983/84 the LCS system handled just under 33 million transactions – an average of 140,000 per day. LCS functions with a total 558 terminals in service.

Supplementing both ILLINET and LCS in Illinois, the Inter–systems Library Delivery Service (ILDS) was initiated in 1980 to facilitate physical access to materials. ILDS provides direct pick–up and delivery services each day, Monday through Friday, to the eighteen Systems, the four R and R Centers, and the three Special Resource Centers. Six routes with interconnecting links have been laid out so that materials can be delivered in one to two days in most instances. ILDS has been centrally funded by the State Library, thus providing appreciable savings of postage or UPS costs for individual libraries. The next step being discussed in Illinois is the development of a cooperative collection development program, and a committee has recently been constituted to study and make recommendations in this area.

The programs and systems which have been described show how libraries have tried and succeeded to a large degree in meeting the challenge of providing greater access to collections. But, librarians also face serious dilemmas in these efforts. It has been suggested, for instance, that we need to think more about collection development at regional and national levels, rather than at the level of individual institutions. Yet, in this regard several questions quickly come to mind. Are libraries ready and willing to direct a portion of their acquisitions budgets to purchase materials for a central repository collection? Is there a feeling that cooperative collection development will, in time, compromise the integrity of already strong collections at some institutions? Will faculty members accept greater reliance upon interlibrary borrowing for the kinds of resources they have been used to obtaining on their respective campuses? Is there assurance that collections at a central repository will be maintained at sufficient levels of strength to satisfy specialized research needs?

One major research library director's response to some of these issues was expressed last year in a forum concerning the future of the Center for Research Libraries. "Although the Center's collections are large and extensive," he wrote, "it is only in a very, very few areas that they are sufficiently comprehensive to be relied upon by North American research libraries, to the point where libraries can discontinue collection development in specific fields of publication. The very real possibility that research libraries will be required to devote a larger share of acquisition budgets to the Center – if they are to continue membership – is untenable unless those libraries can be assured that the CRL collections in categories of some significance are comprehensive, and that they will be maintained at that level."[7] While many librarians favored the proposal several years ago to establish a National Periodicals Center in the United States, the failure of that effort to gain sufficient support may indicate that a middle ground is called for which assures the benefits of cooperation in collection development but does not jeopardize the ability of individual research libraries to provide accurate bibliographical access and efficient physical access for their clientele. The RLG Conspectus appears to offer much hope as a means of identifying areas of present strength and future responsibility in collection development. The availability of bibliographical information in the data bases of major utilities, such as RLIN and OCLC, and the benefits of interlibrary delivery systems, such as the one operating in Illinois, hold further promise that access to collections will be greatly improved as we look to the future.

Reference Services

If a distinguished collection is the heart of an academic or research library, reference service provides the pulse that gives the collection life and vitality. Reference service establishes the necessary link between the recorded knowledge which is contained in the collection, and the users who are seeking information for a variety of reasons and in an endless range of subject fields. Thus, the reference librarian helps in identifying needed items and locating them in the collection; in checking citations that will lead to information sources; in referring to appropriate indexes and bibliographies, and interpreting data entries; in conducting searches using both published works and data bases to locate appropriate resources; in offering instruction individually and in groups; in compiling information for brochures, handbooks and guides; in selecting appropriate works for the collection and offering advice more broadly in the area of collection development; and in observing, surveying and analyzing relevant activities which affect the library's users. As Rogers and Weber observed, "there are relatively few limitations on the extent of reference help, other than availability of staff time."[8]

Some form of reference service has probably existed wherever library and archive collections have been assembled, staffed, and made available for people to use. But, reference service as we now think of it has mainly developed during the last century. Library historians frequently refer to 1876, when Samuel Swett Green published his paper, "Personal Relations between Librarians and Readers," as the time when reference service gained formal recognition. During the years since then many other concerned librarians have recognized the importance of "that phase of library work which is directly concerned with assistance to readers in securing information and in using the resources of the library in study and research," as the *A.L.A. Glossary of Library Terms* describes it.[9]

Reference services have sometimes been categorized as "direct," such as providing information in response to questions and offering instruction to users, or "indirect," including developing reference aids and preparing bibliographies. These differences, however, have become somewhat submerged with the development of a view that the "reference process" is really the core of effective service. According to Alan M. Rees, the reference process "comprises a complex interaction among the questioner, reference librarian, and information sources, involving not only the identification and manipulation of available bibliographic apparatus, but also the operation of psychological, sociological and environmental variables which are imperfectly understood at the present time."[10] In this view the reference function is seen as considerably more complex and sophisticated than just answering questions, because the reasons for which information is being sought and the context in which it is to be used are taken into consideration. In promoting access, the reference librarian is challenged therefore to develop skills not only about bibliographic and information sources, but also about how to communicate, in order to identify the elements that have relevance to the inquirer's information needs. These elements may include the motivation for seeking assistance, the objectives to be met, the way in which information is to be used, and whether a relationship can be perceived between the user's frame of reference and various forms in which knowledge may be organized and discovered. In this setting the reference interview becomes very important in terms of the exchange of ideas, the search for understanding, and the interaction of minds engaged in a process of exploration. The reference interview must be open and uninhibited, free from preconceptions, and altruistic. To the extent that it is possible, nothing artificial should be imposed that may misdirect the process of inquiry and response.

In addition to cultivating the interview technique, providing bibliographic instruction offers a challenge for improving user access. While in the past most academic libraries offered orientation tours or lectures for users, and some tried to promote library instruction as a part of basic courses in required subjects, during the past ten to fifteen years interest in this aspect of reference service has increased greatly. Credit courses have been developed at many institutions based upon an established syllabus and including reference problems, training in compiling bibliographies, writing papers involving search techniques, and taking formal examinations. In some instances, basic level courses are supplemented by more advanced instruction in special subject fields or broad subject areas, such as the humanities, social studies, and physical and life sciences. Conferences on the subject of bibliographic instruction have been held annually for a number of years at Eastern Michigan University in connection with that institution's Library Orientation–Instruction Exchange (LOEX), and programs or seminars have also been held at a number of other institutions and at professional conferences. Recognition of the need to advance bibliographic instruction came when the Association of College and Research Libraries established the Bibliographic Instruction Section in 1977 and issued guidelines to assist institutions in developing programs. Further recognition has been given for a number of years by the feature section on "Library Instruction," edited by Carolyn Kirkendall in the *Journal of Academic Librarianship*. Increasing use of computers in libraries and the availability of data bases for searches provide a new dimension for library instruction programs as we look to the future.

While bibliographical searching has been an important aspect of reference services for many years, the use of computer terminals to perform online searches of data bases has greatly changed this aspect of reference work and offered another challenge to the reference librarian. The availability of commercially operated data bases, such as those maintained by the Lockheed Corporation, Systems Development Corporation (SDC), and Bibliographic Retrieval Services (BRS), has greatly facilitated access to vast amounts of information in many formats. Other systems, such as MEDLINE, operated by the National Library of Medicine, and the Educational Resources Information Center (better known as ERIC), funded by the federal government, have been vital and growing sources for improving access to information. The data bases maintained by the major library networks and utilities, such as the Research Library Information Network (RLIN), based at Stanford University, and the Online Computer Library Center (OCLC), located in Ohio, have also proven to be invaluable aids in providing access to resources.

Two special developments in the online searching field have recently been announced. First, the National Library of Medicine indicated recently that subsets of its data will be available offline in a distributed processing mode, using tapes or floppy disks for libraries to store and re–use information when needed. Second, the Albert R. Mann Library at Cornell University has recently established 'Quicksearch' in order "to provide computer–generated bibliographies at very low cost to undergraduates."[11] This service is designed to meet needs where a comprehensive bibliography is not required and the number of citations is limited to those most highly relevant to the search subject, and to materials in English only. According to librarians at Cornell, the chief value of Quick–search is in offering more comprehensive subject searching than is available through card catalogs or printed indexes.

Improving subject searching is probably the greatest current challenge in promoting access to library collections and information sources. The limitations of subject headings as they have been used for many years in catalogs and indexes is well documented and known by most librarians from firsthand experience. Because terminology changes and words take on different meanings as new concepts emerge, old headings become less useful in representing the intellectual content of collections for new generations of scholars. For reasons of economy and practicality, merely increasing the number of headings is not helpful in the long run. Instead, by means of skillful program designs, computer supported systems that will facilitate extensive cross referencing of subject and index headings with key terms that represent the intellectual contents of materials, offer the best hope for improving and facilitating access. Both the Washington Library Network (WLN) and RLIN systems represent positive moves in this direction. In the process of developing these systems, however, reference librarians need to work with people responsible for cataloging and indexing materials to provide recommendations based upon direct knowledge of users' problems and needs. Moreover, if we are to be successful in these efforts it will be necessary also for a balance to be achieved between theoretical analyses of knowledge and practical uses of information.

At this point in considering the impact of reference services on access to resources we begin to see dilemmas as well as challenges before us. Will sufficient financial resources be available to develop the kinds of programs and services that are needed? Although consumers have improved the ways libraries function, they have not saved money. Moreover, while libraries have traditionally provided materials and services without fees, in areas such as online bibliographic searching the question arises about who pays for accessing data bases. While relying more heavily upon electrostatic copies and reprints to satisfy users' demands, how far will libraries go in diverting funds from purchases for the collection to supporting the free dissemination of requested items? As new sources for information and access tools become increasingly complicated, and as computer-based systems multiply, will librarians be able to keep abreast of new developments or will their training be sufficient for only one or two decades in the profession? Although libraries have long relied upon interlibrary borrowing and resource sharing to supplement their own resources, can librarians and users adapt to a new scenario in which dependence upon resources at remote locations increases, as the ability of local collections to support research needs decreases? While these questions are not asked to discourage progress, they do need to be faced and resolved if reference services are to contribute positively in improving access to information and library collections.

Preservation

The subject of preserving library materials is quite different from either collection development or reference services in terms of its impact upon access to collections. Whereas access is associated with making materials readily available and promoting their use, preservation represents a more conservative approach in terms of protecting, saving and, if need be, restricting use of materials. This difference was pointed out by Richard M. Dougherty in an editorial for the *Journal of Academic Librarianship*. "The objectives of library preservation programs are not in harmony with the objectives of access policies and resource sharing programs. Preservation programs strive to reduce usage and handling; access policies and resource sharing programs are intended to encourage use of materials."[12] Yet, because both access and preservation represent viable needs, efforts must be made to resolve the potential conflict between them.

Concern for preservation of library and archival materials is not a recent development. The very fact that people have been recording and saving information from earliest times attests to an interest in preserving knowledge and transmitting it from one generation to another. In fact, when one takes the long view it also becomes clear that interest in preservation was not solely for archival purposes; materials were preserved so that future generations would have access to information sources, thereby assuring the continuation of civilized societies. In this sense, we can see preservation and access not in conflict, but as directed toward a common purpose.

While widespread conversion from rag content to pulp paper in the last third of the nineteenth century has generally been viewed as the turning point in the deterioration of library materials, as early as 1823, John Murray expressed concern in England about "the present state of the wretched compound called *Paper.*"[13] The problem of fungi attacking paper was the subject of a dissertation by Pierre Seé, a French mycologist, in 1919. In the United States during the fifties and sixties, William J. Barrow conducted experiments on the useful life of paper and predicted that many books published before 1950 would not be usable in the twenty–first century. The Arno River flood which extensively damaged collections in the Biblioteca Nazionale Centrale in Florence, Italy, and the fire which destroyed about half the collection at the Jewish Theological Seminary in New York City, in 1966, raised the consciousness of librarians to the potential dangers of natural disasters. About this time the Library of Congress established its Preservation Office, and shortly afterward the New York Public Library created a Conservation Division to address collection maintenance and preservation concerns.

John P. Baker, who has headed the program at the New York Public Library since 1972, points out a number of aspects related to conservation/preservation activities that need to be kept in mind.[14] It is a highly technical field because of the interaction of chemistry, the environment, and book structures. There are unresolved ethical and philosophical questions which affect conservation/preservation decisions for which answers are needed. Consideration needs to be given to the comparative importance of preserving materials for their artifact value versus preserving their intellectual contents. Because deterioration and decay are well advanced in many collections, the scope of the problem and the press of time add to the seriousness of the situation. Conservation/ preservation activities are expensive and libraries need to determine how far they can go in allocating funds for this purpose. The scarcity of trained conservators and the slowness in developing treatment standards are reminders that this is still a young and developing field. Finally, viewing preservation and conservation of collections as a national problem, cooperative programs need to be established if our library resources are to be saved.

Lest we feel overwhelmed at this point, it is important to say (as is often done when emergencies arise), "Help is on the way." Considerable progress has been made in single institution and regional conservation/preservation centers, such as the Library of Congress, the Newberry Library, the Northeast Document Conservation Center, and the Illinois and Midwest Cooperative Conservation Centers located at Southern Illinois University in Carbondale. The formal education and training program instituted at Columbia University under the leadership of Pamela Darling offers great promise in terms of preparing conservationists to work in libraries. For librarians and library administrators who want to learn more about this field, I would strongly recommend two books both authored by Carolyn Clark Morrow: *The Preservation Challenge: A Guide to Conserving Library Materials,* published in 1983 by Knowledge Industry Publications, Inc., of White Plains, New York; and *Conservation Treatment Procedures: A Manual of Step--by-- Step Procedures for the Maintenance and Repair of Library Mater-- ials,* published in 1982 by Libraries Unlimited, Inc., of Littleton, Colorado.[15]

In order for preservation activities to have a positive impact upon access to collections, libraries should develop what are com-- monly referred to as "phased programs." This means that, instead of assuming a library can launch a comprehensive program from the start, consideration will be given to the gradual development and phasing in of reasonable conservation/preservation activities. The first step is to survey the collections to determine the degree to which deterioration and decay have already become problems. Usually the situation is more serious for older libraries where there are large holdings of materials over fifty years of age. But, relatively young libraries which have acquired older collections may also discover serious problems. The second step is to make plans that take into consideration what can be done to retard the deterioration process, how preventive maintenance can be achieved, and the degree to which resources will be available for treatment and restora-- tion services. Then, realistic proposals should be incorporated into an overall program which describes the library's preservation/ conservation goals and objectives, and indicates how they can be achieved.

There are many things that all libraries can do to meet basic preservation needs. Consideration should be given to environmental elements, such as temperature and humidity control, and amounts of light and dust, which affect the collections. Attention to common practices, such as handling materials and providing appropriate shelving or other means of storage, proper methods for cleaning and repairing, avoiding use of tapes or glue that have long--term damaging effects, and applying appropriate dressings for leather-- bound books, is important. In writing binding specifications libraries should be aware of potentially dangerous practices and should specify provisions that will protect and add to the useful life of materials. Care should be exercised in the selection of copying machines to avoid those which necessitate applying pressure and thereby weaken book bindings. Many libraries should consider developing brittle--books programs where volumes showing signs of advanced deterioration are placed in protective cases, or given restoration treatment, or replaced by microform copies.

Preparing a policy statement is an important aspect of developing a conservation/preservation program because it clarifies the library's goals and objectives, describes the levels of activities which will be undertaken, and establishes lines of authority and responsibility for decisions and specific tasks. Closely related to, or part of the policy statement, should be a description of how the library will prepare for, and cope with, a potential disaster such as flooding, fire and smoke damage, or infestation. The ideal is for libraries to establish, equip and operate their own preservation treatment centers; but, costs are very high and adequately trained conservators and conservation technicians are not readily available to staff these centers. In many cases contracting for services from a commercial firm or a cooperative agency offers a more realistic way for libraries to satisfy treatment needs.

In terms of their effects upon access to collection, conservation/preservation activities need to be the focus for cooperative efforts within states, regions and the nation. Every library has a stake in preserving materials and we cannot afford to assume someone else will solve the problem for us. In addition to the programs already operating in many areas, much attention needs to be given to preservation microfilming activities, such as those in which the RLG libraries are already well advanced. Besides improving physical access through microfilming, however, it will be equally important to establish comprehensive ways to assure bibliographic access so that those who need materials will know where to find them. Looking to the future the potential benefits of optical disk storage programs, such as the one currently being developed at the Library of Congress, offer much hope for preserving the intellectual content of research materials. Finally, working through library associations and governmental agencies where possible efforts to encourage publishers to increase use of acid–free papers are an important part of the conservation/preservation process which cannot be ignored.

Preservation, then, offers many challenges and dilemmas. Given realistic proposals, thoughtfully conceived programs, and sufficient support, the challenges can be met. Meeting and overcoming the dilemmas involves balancing the short term needs for quick and easy access to materials, with the long term concerns for assuring access to generations of users yet to come. Through the application of sound and reasonable conservation/preservation practices, through thoughtful and prudent judgements, and with adequate financial support, we have reason to feel confident that conscientious librarians will resolve many of the potential conflicts in these areas.

Conclusion

We have seen that efforts to improve access to library resources present both challenges and dilemmas in relation to collection development, reference services, and preservation. It has also been apparent that, in each of these areas, while retaining useful policies and procedures from the past, academic librarians will need continually to look to the future in developing new ways to improve access to scholarly information. Several qualities or characteristics on the part of librarians and library administrators are needed if we are to meet the challenges and resolve the dilemmas.

The first one is flexibility. It will be important for us to avoid the pitfalls of rigid policies and procedures, and unwillingness to accept changes. It is easy to fall into the "This is the way we have always done it" syndrome, or to say, "If it isn't broken, don't try to fix it." The facts are that changes are occurring all about us in society, and libraries cannot afford to stand still. Modern technology and especially the computer have vastly affected almost every aspect of our lives and, as has already been pointed out, they have greatly affected library operations. We cannot afford to rest in an "either/or" frame of mind between the comfortable, tried and true ways of the past, and the uncertain yet exciting possibilities for the future. Instead, we must try wherever possible to use the best from the past, while adapting it to new ways of the future. Flexibility is the ability to adapt and accept change; it is also one of the marks of professional growth.

Second, we need clear insight into the role of libraries as conser-vators of knowledge and providers of information. It is important that we try continually to understand the needs of our clientele, and to see the development of collections, or the requests for infor-mation from the standpoint of the user. At the ACRL national conference in Seattle last April, one of the speakers, the president of a major American university, cautioned his audience about the dangers of becoming self--serving. Thus, in selecting materials, providing services, and developing procedures by which libraries operate, we must look beyond ourselves to understand the larger community which it is our mission to serve.

Finally, the decisions we make must be based upon informed judgements concerning the issues at hand. While it is easy to develop opinions and to hold certain views strongly, it is most important that we keep open minds and reasonable attitudes in weighing matters before us. Obtaining the facts, considering options, discuss-ing alternatives, and making decisions free from personal prejudices -- these elements are necessary to benefit the institutions and people we serve. It is within this framework that we can best face the issues of access to library collections and scholarly information, and deal with them not as dilemmas but as challenges.

NOTES

1. "Access Innovations, Inc. Buys NICEM Audiovisual Index Service," *Library Journal*, vol. 109:13 (August 1984), p. 1382.

2. *ALA Handbook of Organization, 1983/84.* Chicago: American Library Association, 1983. p. 6.

3. Patricia Battin, "The Library: Center of the Restructured University," *College & Research Libraries*, vol. 45:3 (May 1984), p. 172.

4. Dorothy A. Koenig, "Rushmore at Berkeley: The Dynamics of Developing a Written Collections Policy Statement," *Journal of Academic Librarianship*, vol. 7:6 (January 1982), p. 344.

5. Y.T. Feng, "The Necessity for a Collection Development Policy Statement," *Library Resources and Technical Services*, vol. 23:1 (Winter 1979), p. 43.

6. Nancy E. Gwinn and Paul H. Mosher, "Coordinating Collection Development: The RLG Conspectus," *College and Research Libraries*, vol. 44:2 (March 1983), pp. 128–40.

7. Joseph A. Rosenthal, "Toward a Viable Program for CRL -- Back to Basics," *Journal of Academic Librarianship*, vol. 9:5 (November 1983), p. 269.

8. Rutherford D. Rogers and David C. Weber, *University Library Administration.* New York: H.W. Wilson, Co., 1971. p. 202.

9. Elizabeth H. Thompson, *A.L.A. Glossary of Library Terms.* Chicago: American Library Association, 1943. p. 113.

10. Alan M. Rees, "Broadening the Spectrum." In Winifred B. Linderman, ed., *The Present Status and Future Prospects of Reference/Information Service.* Chicago: American Library Association, 1967. p. 58.

11. James Markiewicz and Linda Guyotte Stewart, "Quicksearch: Computer Searching for Undergraduates at Cornell University," *Journal of Academic Librarianship*, vol. 10:3 (July 1984), p. 134.

12. Richard M. Dougherty, "Editorial – Preservation and Access:

A Collision of Objectives," *Journal of Academic Librarianship,* vol. 8:4 (September 1982), p. 199.

13. John P. Baker, "Conservation and Preservation of Library Materials." In *ALA World Encyclopedia of Library and Information Services.* Chicago: American Library Association, 1980. p. 161.

14. *Ibid.*

15. Carolyn Clark Morrow, *The Preservation Challenge: A Guide to Conserving Library Materials.* White Plains, N.Y.: Knowledge Industry Publications, Inc., 1983. 231 pp. Also *Conservation Treatment Procedures: A Manual of Step–by–Step Procedures for the Maintenance and Repair of Library Materials.* Littleton, Colorado: Libraries Unlimited, Inc., 1982. 191 pp.

Recent Developments in Technical Services and their Implications For Access to Scholarly Information

Helen H. Spalding

Library technical services have direct influence upon user services, and thus upon access to information. For a long time, technical services personnel have felt, along with Rodney Dangerfield, that they "don't get no respect." Their feelings are changing as more library administrators and public service librarians become more aware and appreciative of the role bibliographic control plays in providing service to users.

Behind the scenes, the technical services staff in acquisitions, serials, and cataloging departments purchase and place under bibliographic control the material selected for the library's collection. All aspects of the work in these departments affect whether items being processed can be located and used in a timely manner.

Many in the academic community have associated library technical services functions with barriers, rather than avenues, to information access. The card catalog represents a challenge to understand. Sometimes it seems that the filing order, choice of entry, and selection of subject headings defy logic. Online catalogs appear to duplicate many of the limitations of the card catalog, rather than overcoming them. Browsing in the book stacks, researchers may puzzle at the classification of some books together on the shelf. Current material may be easier to borrow from other libraries, than to wait for the placement, receipt, and cataloging of an order in one's own university library.

The goals of bibliographic control are to describe individual packages of information, whether they be books, magazine issues, microfiche, sound recordings, or software disks, so that researchers can locate a specific title, related titles, works by a specific author, or works about a specific subject. It continues to be a complex, labor intensive process that will never result in successful, timely access to all information by any one person.[1]

The access problems related to bibliographic control do not exist because catalogers are ignorant, incompetent, or insensitive to the needs of library users. And they do not exist because of lack of recognition or study of the problems. National economic and political issues dictate the boundaries of what solutions are possible.

Automation of Technical Services

The primary motivation for the introduction of computers to the backroom of the library was the escalating cost of creating and maintaining manual files. Greater fiscal accountability was being asked of higher education administrators, who faced tighter funding and decreasing enrollments in the 1970's. Library budgets began to feel the impact of these pressures. Funds for new building projects, staff, acquisitions, and keeping up with inflation were no longer as abundant.

Developing technology appeared to offer solutions that might slow the rising labor expense of technical services processing. By putting bibliographic information in machine–readable form, shared cataloging and inter–library loan activities could be enhanced. Machine–readable records could be sorted and reproduced auto-matically. Certain information could appear in a record by default, rather than being added by a cataloger in each instance. Records could be shared online or by tape with other institutions, providing more rapid transmission of current information than was possible through printed sources like the *National Union Catalog*. By sharing this information, original cataloging costs supposedly could be reduced. Scholars would view the information available to them as being more than the collection housed at their academic address, reducing their expectations of individual acquisitions budgets.[2]

Most research libraries now perform their cataloging through a shared data base of machine–readable records. The technological opportunities to share cataloging copy, facilitate inter–library loan, and build online catalogs with enhanced access are being realized. But the anticipation of savings in staff positions has not been met.

Standards

Adherence to network standards carries with it the costs of keeping staff training, performance, and documentation current with system norms. Membership and system use fees, computer hardware and telecommunications costs are part of the price of cooperative cataloging and resource–sharing. As online catalogs are developed and implemented, researchers have less patience with the need to search a variety of tools for the information they need. Cataloging departments feel pressure to retrospectively con--

vert the records in their card catalogs to machine–readable form so that patrons need only look in the online catalog for the category of materials they must now search for in the card catalogs as well. As with many of the other problems of access, all it takes are more time and money to complete retrospective conversion of records and to develop sophisticated, automated access tools.

Any material under bibliographic control must conform to standards in format and entry in order for it to be retrieved by the variety of searchers looking for it in different library settings. Authority control, the most expensive aspect of bibliographic control, remains as important, if not more important, in an online environment as it was in card files.[3] One validation of its importance is that it is being discussed outside of technical service conference rooms and RTSD committees, in groups such as the ARL Directors.[4] Persuasive arguments have been made that an imposed consistency through authority control is necessary, especially as data bases of bibliographic information mushroom.[5] The machine– readable format allows for greater manipulation of the information and efficient detection and correction of errors. The questions remaining concern how this authority structure is best maintained and how much authority control is adequate.

Libraries have not been able to throw out completely their older systems each time a new technological advance has offered a more effective solution. Progress has had to be incremental, building on the system of the past and integrating the new. As cooperation among libraries expands, decision–making becomes a shared process, in which time for negotiation and acceptance of compromise retard the ability to take radical new directions. Political issues of governance and economical issues of data base copyright and shared system development add to the complexity of change.

These observations are not excuses, but merely indications of the economic realities in which technical services staffs have had to adjust to change, while maintaining a cohesive system of bibliographic control that will guide users to the information they are seeking.

The most visible relationship of technical services to public access is through the cataloging information displayed in card, COM, book, and online catalogs. At the same time, access is affected indirectly by other technical services functions as well.

Acquisitions and Serials Functions

The size of acquisitions budgets for local purchases remains important. Although online inter–library loan and plans for coop––

erative collection development have opened the walls of research libraries, timeliness of document delivery between libraries remains a problem. One measure of a university's quality continues to be its library collection.

The acquisitions staff can affect the amount and availability of materials by their management of department resources. How cost--effectively the Acquisitions Librarian selects vendors and negotiates discounts and service fees can have an impact on the amount of money available to purchase books. The efficiency of the processing workflow affects the ability of the department to verify and obtain hard to find titles, to avoid duplicate purchases, and to get material on the shelves in time to meet current research needs.

External factors also may affect whether the acquisitions and serials departments can acquire requested titles. Increasing postal rates reduce the money that can be spent on materials, which in turn, may have an impact on the financial viability of smaller pub--lishers, such as university presses. The ability of dealers to ware--house out--of--print books and back issues of serials determines whether items mutilated or stolen by library users can be replaced. Several vendors now offer online inventory searching, or online ordering capability, facilitating order fulfillment. Integrated online catalogs provide public access to on--order and in--process records. With this information, the patron can request notification upon receipt of the item, or rush cataloging.

Depending upon the system, serials information also can be centralized and made available online to the public, allowing users to view the location of the latest issue checked in, as well as the earlier volumes and issues received. Certainly, such systems have been a blessing to the staffs who remember laboriously updating check--in, invoice, binding, and summary holdings information in different manual files that also may have been duplicated at other locations in the library system.

Many times, the need to streamline the processing files has served as the basis for current online catalog systems now in use. The NOTIS software has built upon an initial automated serials check--in system. Some libraries are developing online catalog access from automated circulation systems.

Serials union lists facilitate resource sharing, and are being produced from information placed in shared data bases, such as OCLC. These cooperative lists may reflect a geographic region or a category of materials, such as law materials.

Cataloging

46

Regardless of the impact of other technical services functions on the availability of research material, cataloging is the area that receives the most attention in relation to public access. For years, catalogers have suffered being stereotyped as champions of filing rules no one can follow, creators of subject headings no one uses, and conjurors of the mysterious cataloging rules. Rather than being seen as the facilitators of access to information, catalogers often have been viewed as troublesome nitpickers, who have placed impediments in the path of service.

Most of today's librarians have lived through the implementation of AACR2. The goals of the second edition of the *Anglo--American Cataloging Rules* were innocent enough: to consolidate the 1967 North American and British texts, add material updated since 1967, and encourage the international adoption of the tool. Certainly, these objectives would facilitate the international exchange of information.[6]

As we know, the implementation of the new rules was an expensive proposition that directly affected access to information. The greatest impact of the new edition was in the changes made to many headings. Most libraries could not afford to pull the card sets and change them to conform to the new forms of headings mandated by the new rules. Instead, cross reference systems were put in place, linking old and new forms of entry as discrepancies arose. Some libraries followed the Library of Congress's example of freezing the card catalog containing pre--AACR2 cataloging entries and opening a new card catalog that followed the new code. Researchers had to learn more about cataloging entry, look under more than one form of heading or in more than one file, or ask for help.

The natural confusion of cataloging format and filing order that existed in card catalogs before AACR2 was compounded by these random split files. The online catalog developments in progress began to take on a new sheen as librarians involved in their planning saw the means to overcome the increasingly frustrating limitations of the card catalog. New impetus was added to retrospective conversion efforts, so that implementation of the online catalog could result in the simultaneous death of the card catalog.

For all the imperfection of the Library of Congress classification system and subject headings, the Dewey Decimal classification system, and the *Anglo--American Cataloguing Rules,* librarians have been grateful for their existence and availability. Using these conventions has been cheaper than the invention of new, although possibly better, systems. Library supervisors and library school professors can provide a general, broad based introduction to these systems and know that the training will be relevant, in a variety of institutions to the work in which their charges will soon find themselves. Prior to the creating of large online data bases like OCLC, RLIN, and WLN, research libraries saved in–house original cataloging costs by using the cataloging copy from the Library of Congress or other research libraries, through the *National Union Catalog.*

Automation was expected to enhance the ability of libraries not only to share their materials and cataloging, but also to create new avenues of access information. Technologically, this rational theory was sound. Economically, librarians are finding that without unlimited funds, we must continue to build on what we have, even if what we have is not perfect.

Online catalog transaction logs may show that users search for information very differently than we now believe they do. Their use of online catalogs will teach us more about what access points are really used and wanted. Even with this information, we are constrained by what our budget allows us to do. Because users want free–text searching, Boolean capability, and the ability to specify when search terms are sequential, will we be able to afford to meet these needs?

Certainly, the machine–readable records are easier to change, manipulate, and transmit to other libraries than 3 x 5 manually typed cards. But sharing information with other institutions re–quires that all adhere to common standards. If unscrambling and translating information from other libraries were necessary before it could be used, the chief efficiencies of shared information would be lost.

The formulation, modification, and enforcement of standards is not an inexpensive process. Although the Library of Congress is not formally responsible for the creation of standards for bib–liographic control, it has made economic sense for research libraries to follow the Library of Congress's cataloging practice. By using the MARC II format, LC or Dewey Decimal classification, LC subject headings, and the *Anglo-American Cataloguing Rules,* online or tape transfer of useable cataloging information among research libraries has been facilitated and duplication of work reduced.

New formats of information, such as computer software, and new areas of research have evolved since the establishment of these well–known conventions. With no national agency officially respon–sible for the monitoring, changing, and disseminating of cataloging standards, revision and updating of methods and standards of bib–liographic control may follow far behind the recognition of the need for change. But supplementary cataloging rules and new subject headings eventually find their way into the complex array of cataloging guides.

New technical capabilities for controlling bibliographic informa–
tion, and a climate of cooperation, have made library technical
services operations more visible in the effort to provide access to
information, nationwide. The development and use of national
data bases and local online catalogs have led to more mutual aware–
ness of and appreciation for the diverse contributions all library
employees make to library services, in spite of limited resources.

Let me share with you some other recent activities that build
on the accomplishments of the past and facilitate the ability of
libraries to locate and share resources.

Minimal Level Cataloging

Because full, original cataloging continues to be an expensive
process, research libraries are considering the creation of minimal
level records for certain types of material. The Library of Congress
has begun doing so for microform analytics, some serials, and some
backlog materials. The University of Illinois–Urbana, Columbia,
University of California--Berkeley, UCLA, and Stanford have varying
practices that result in minimal level records.[7]

Justification for less than full cataloging is based on several
points. Given the staffing workloads in most cataloging departments,
some material of lower priority would never get cataloged if it
had to wait for full cataloging. Some access is better than none
for these titles. If online catalogs are able to supply key word access
to records in an online data base, the minimal level records may
have more information for their retrieval than full records do now in
the card catalog, although several added entries and subject headings
would not be supplied in the minimal level records.

Controversy centers on what criteria separate titles into the
category of minimal level cataloging; whether the records should
be used only in--house, or shared in national data bases; the impact
of providing only limited access points; and whether the records
are adequate to allow verification of a unique item.[8]

Retrospective Conversion

Minimal level cataloging is discussed in the area of retrospective
conversion, as well as in relation to new titles being cataloged.
Retrospective conversion of records in the card catalog to machine--
readable form can be an expensive project. The OCLC and RLIN
data bases contain primarily imprints of the last twenty years,
so cataloging copy is not available online for most older titles.
Many older records in card catalogs are brief, and of course, do
not follow current cataloging practice. Retrospective conversion

often means recataloging completely the older material. Recata--
loging is a costly process, especially when viewed in terms of the
usually limited cataloging staff available to catalog new acquisitions.
Minimal level cataloging offers a less expensive route, although
many catalogers feel it is an inadvisable one, due to the lesser quality
of these records.[9]

Libraries have many alternative avenues for converting records
retrospectively. They can do the work in--house, relying on a
national data base such as OCLC for cataloging copy, or use one
of the rapidly growing regional data bases. At the University of
Missouri, the combined data base of OCLC records from the four
campuses totals over 600,000. The smaller campuses are able to
convert as much as a third of their records using this university--
wide data base, by simply attaching their holdings to a record already
supplied by another UM campus.

More retrospective conversion options are available outside
the library. OCLC and regional library networks, such as AMIGOS,
will contract to perform the retrospective conversion for a library,
and include customized editing to bring records up to OCLC input
standards, while entering them into the OCLC data base. Private
corporations will provide converted records on tape to libraries,
based on the information the library supplies the companies. Record
quality and completeness vary with the data base used and the
level of project staff. Of course, the more retrospective conversion
being done, the larger the cataloging data bases grow, resulting
in more records for other libraries to use in their conversion projects.

Non--book Formats

Although the problems of direct, centralized access to mono--
graphs and serials seem overwhelming, the problems of access to
other types of information are even greater.

Computer software needs to be housed and put under bibliogra--
phic control so that it can be used by researchers as yet another
source of information. The American Library Association's new
publication, *Guidelines for Using AACR2, Chapter 9 for Cataloging
Microcomputer Software,* provides supplementary information
to catalogers dealing with this relatively new format.[10] Concur--
rently, a new MARC format for machine--readable data files is
being developed so that the cataloging records can be input into
national data bases of MARC records.

Access to data files that must be loaded on large main frame
computers remains a problem. Usually these files, such as the
U.S. Census tapes, are housed and used in campus computer centers.
The role of libraries in providing bibliographic access and service

50

to these files is unclear.[11]   Use of these files often requires quanti--
tative skills, especially in the area of statistical analysis.   If the
information is available only on computer tape, does the library
still view itself as responsible for providing the professional assistance
necessary to gain access to, understand, and use this information?

Information in a micro-format does not always receive the
bibliographic control it needs to insure access.   The second edition
of AACR stipulated in chapter 11 that a microform edition must
have a cataloging record separate from that of the work in original
form.   The implication is that the form of the work is more impor--
tant than its content.   Rather than noting the microformat on the
cataloging record of the original, catalogers must now completely
describe the reproduction, often with inadequate information
in hand.   Good descriptive cataloging is difficult to provide from
the piece itself when one must depend upon the leader of a micro--
film, or the abbreviated information appearing on a box or enve--
lope.[12]   A simple solution is to stockpile the pieces in the cataloging backlog where they are often out of sight and out of mind.

The Association of Research Libraries (ARL) tackled another
aspect of information in a micro-format.   Many titles are being
republished in microform sets.   As an example, *Eighteenth--Century
Sources for the Study of English Literature and Culture* is a set
containing over 1400 titles, on over 264 reels.   Clearly, scholars
need guidance in using these sets.   Some micropublishers supply
lists or cards to use as guides to the sets, but often these are not
adequate descriptions, and do not conform to cataloging standards
that would allow them to be interfiled with regular cataloging
information.   Libraries attempting to catalog these sets themselves
are making a tremendous investment not only in creating the thousands of catalog records, but also possibly in time needed to file
the cards sets in their card catalogs.[13]

ARL recognized the general waste of resources that would
result if several research libraries attempted to catalog the same
monstrous sets, and realized that most libraries were not able to
provide any access to the sets.[14]   Their alternative was to establish
the ARL Microform Project Clearinghouse.   Through a survey,
the Project compiled information on collections being republished
in micro-formats, and how research libraries are providing bibliographic control for them.   Libraries can contact the Clearinghouse
to discover what titles already have been cataloged by other libraries,
what titles are being cataloged, and the national data base in which
the cataloging records have been entered.

The Project has encouraged the development of standards for
cataloging and preserving microforms, and has made their machine--
readable cataloging records available to all research libraries, through

the major bibliographic utilities.

As part of its preservation program, the Library of Congress is experimenting with the storage of material on laser video disks and digital audio disks. At the completion of the Optical Disk Pilot Program, scholars will be able to locate the stored materials through a computerized catalog. At present, no MARC format for cataloging records of visual images exists, but the records created for the optical disks may serve as a basis for a new MARC format that will be needed by other libraries. Materials from LC's Prints and Photographs Division, and Motion Picture, Broadcasting and Recorded Sound Division will be reproduced on disks during the project, greatly enhancing their preservation and access.[15]

CLR Supported Projects

Researchers are turning their attention to the potential differ-ences in user expectations of and system capabilities for access to bibliographic information through online catalogs. The Council on Library Resources (CLR) has been a leader in encouraging pro-gress in these areas.

In 1978, the Council established the Bibliographic Services Development Program (BSDP) to focus attention on the need for improved standards, access to bibliographic information, linkage of bibliographic data bases, name authority, subject authority, and bibliographic data base products and services. Its charge was to encourage "cooperation among the major producers of bibliogra-phic records . . . to facilitate implementation of a nationwide bib-liographic network," and to "reduce the economic, technical and organizational constraints on access to information."[16]

BSDP advisory committees review AACR2 rule interpretations and MARC formats. Support is provided to the serials project, CONSER, to encourage use and expansion of its data base. The major abstracting and indexing services in the United States and Canada are entering into CONSER the serials to which they provide access, and the Government Printing Office is authenticating U.S. federal documents in the data base. CONSER is available through the OCLC data base on tape from the Library of Congress. New Serial Titles is generated from the CONSER data base.[17]The CONSER data base also is being expanded by grants from the National Endow-ment for the Humanities (NEH), that are supporting the input of bibliographic records from six major newspaper collections.

The two best known BSDP efforts have been the Online Public Access Catalog Project (OPAC), and the Standard Network Inter-connection (SNI). The two--year online catalog project participants surveyed in 1981 the users and nonusers in libraries with seventeen very different online catalog systems. Despite the wide variation of systems, several common reactions to the systems were found. The user and nonusers were positive about online catalogs, and believed they were better than card catalogs. Even if they did not find the material for which they were searching, they were satisfied with the information they found. Patrons have problems with the online catalog's command structure and want records for more types of material added to the data base. Over half of the searches were by subject.[18] This project will be the basis for future research related to improving the ability of patrons to use online catalogs and the ability of online catalogs to provide needed information. Subject analysis and access are areas of particular interest. Already, the Council has awarded a grant for study of the Dewey Decimal classification system, as a possible enhancement of subject access in online public catalogs.[19]

The Standard Network Interconnection Project is trying to find the technical answers to the fact that users of a specific bibliographic utility do not have access to records in other large data bases. Link-- ing the major data bases through internetwork connections would create a national bibliographic data base, greatly improving access to library materials. The Washington Library Network (WLN), RLG, and LC, with OCLC an observer, are participating in the development of the telecommunications protocols required to search and retrieve information among the systems.

Concurrently, the Linked Systems Project (LSP) is dealing with the problems involved in linking the authority files of WLN, RLG, LC, and OCLC. The Council's Task Force on a Name Author-- ity File Service (NAFS) performed work early in this project, ad-- vising the Library of Congress on standards for authority records. The Name Authority File Cooperative (NACO) Project at LC in-- cludes twenty--four institutions who contribute authority records to the Library of Congress name authority file.[20]

Other Categories of Material

The Cataloging Department provides bibliographic control for those materials that the library catalogs. Government publications often are uncataloged and thus do not always receive the visibility they should. Now, access to government documents has been enhanced. The Government Printing Office now catalogs the docu-- ments it publishes and this information is available on MARC tapes, which are added regularly to the large data bases of the bibliographic utilities.

Western scholars always have had troubles retrieving information on research material that is published in nonroman form. Many times, the cataloging records for these works have been romanized, which can alter the meaning. Interfiling romanized and nonromanized records in card catalogs could mislead searchers by the cards' sequence. In the last few years, technology has answered some of the problems of bibliographic control of nonroman titles.

Telex has developed a terminal that can handle the entire ALA/MARC character set.[21] OCLC and Asiagraphics are working on a word processor support package that will display nonroman characters on the M300 Workstation, a converted IBM personal computer.[22]

The greatest strides in this area have been taken by the Research Libraries Group (RLG). In 1979, the Library of Congress agreed to cooperate with RLG on the development of the technology needed for bibliographic control of Chinese, Japanese, and Korean records. The result, in the summer of 1983, was a $34,000 "CJK" terminal, built by Transtech International Corporation. Development of this terminal also led to the expansion of the MARC format so that it could include both romanized and CJK information.

Several large East Asian collections have purchased the CJK terminals and are putting their records into RLIN. The University of Toronto has loaded 100,000 pre–1983 romanized records into the RLIN data base, and they can now be upgraded by adding the information in the original vernacular. In addition to the efforts of research libraries, the Project Asia of Los Angeles is cataloging Chinese, Japanese, Korean, and Vietnamese books for five California public library systems.[23] Both RLG and OCLC intend to work on Cyrillic, Hebrew, and Arabic displays.

Another category of material that has little visibility outside of individual collections is that of archives and manuscripts. OCLC provides input formats and standards for manuscript material. This year, RLIN implemented support for archives and manuscripts in its system. Access to these materials through the two largest bibliographic utilities will result in greater availability for research.

Final Comments

The entire library organization is involved in decisions to automate or become involved in the cooperative projects that are enhancing access to scholarly information. These decisions lead to more involvement across division lines, perhaps even in complete reorganization of divisions, as public services and technical services librarians share information to gain mutual understanding of the creation and use of authority information and access points. Relationships outside the library are taking on new form as well. Sud–

denly, other libraries not only have access to materials in your library, but they may even be suggesting how you might manage internal resources, particularly in relation to a cooperative project.

The complexity of these new interdependents is a part of the challenge facing management in the control of technological change. Administrators must examine their resources and plan carefully in advance, recognizing the problems of adaptation in the direction of both human and material resources. Technical problems consist not only of learning and operating a system, but also of planning for the most efficient use of shared technology to achieve the full potential of the system within the local context.

The growth of national cooperation to meet the needs of re-searchers is evidenced in each of the recent technical services developments mentioned above. Through cooperation, many problems in access that we face today will have solutions in the future.

REFERENCES

1. Stephen Van Houten, "In the Iron Age of Cataloging," *Library Resources & Technical Services* 25 (October/December 1981): 362–373.

2. "Research Library Collection in a Changing Universe: Four Points of View," *College & Research Libraries* 45 (May 1984): 214–224.

3. Larry Auld, "Authority Control: An Eighty–Year Review," *Library Resources & Technical Services* 26 (October/December 1982), p. 320.

4. *Minutes of the 103rd Meeting: The Sum of the Parts: Sharing the Responsibility for Bibliographic Control* (Washington, D.C.: Association of Research Libraries, 1984).

5. Henriette D. Avram, "Authority Control and Its Place," *Journal of Academic Librarianship* 9 (January 1984), pp. 331–335.

6. *Anglo–American Cataloguing Rules,* 2nd ed., edited by Michael Gorman and Paul W. Winkler. (Chicago: American Library Association, 1978), pp. vi–vii.

7. Colleen Bednar, "Library Exchange," *RTSD Newsletter* 8 (March/April 1983), p. 21.

8. Olivia Madison, "OCLC Cataloging Advisory Committee Meeting

Report," *Action for Libraries* 10 (July, 1984), p. 6.

9. Linda F. Crismond, "Quality Issues in Retrospective Conversion Projects," *Library Resources & Technical Services* 25 (January/March 1981), pp. 48–55.

10. *Guidelines for Using AACR2, Chapter 9 for Cataloging Micro-computer Software.* (Chicago: American Library Association, 1984).

11. "Nonbibliographic Machine–Readable Databases in ARL Libraries," SPEC Kit 105 (June 1984).

12. Louis Charles Willard, "Microforms and AACR2, Chapter 11: Is the Cardinal Principle a Peter Principle?" *Microform Review* 10 (Spring 1981), pp. 75–78.

13. Suzanne Cates Dodson, "Bibliographical Control," *Microform Review* 9 (Summer 1980), pp. 145–153.

14. *Cataloging Titles in Microform Sets* (Washington, D.C.: Association of Research Libraries, 1983).

15. Carl Fleischhauer, "Research Access and Use: the Key Facet of the Nonprint Optical Disk Experiment," *LC Information Bulletin* 42 (September 12, 1983), pp. 312–316.

16. "Cooperation for National Bibliographic Service is BSDP Keynote," *CLR Recent Developments* 9 (August 1981), pp. 1–2.

17. Benita M. Weber, "The Year's Work in Serials: 1981," *Library Resources & Technical Services* 26 (July/September 1982), p. 281.

18. Douglas Ferguson, Neal K. Kaske, Gary S. Lawrence, Joseph R. Matthews, and Robert Zich, "The CLR Online Public Catalog Study: An Overview," *Information Technology & Libraries* 1 (June 1981), pp. 84–97.

19. "CLR Awards Forest Press, OCLC $94,350 for Study of Dewey Classification as Online Tool," *Information Technology & Libraries* 3 (June 1984), pp. 209–210.

20. "Work on System Links Progresses," *CLR Recent Developments* 11 (January 1983), pp. 2–3.

21. R. Bruce Miller, "Nonroman Scripts and Computer Terminal Developments," *Information Technology & Libraries* 1 (June 1982), pp. 143–148.

22. "OCLC to Develop Non–Roman Alphabet Capabilities," *Wilson Library Bulletin* 58 (January 1984), p. 330.

23. Russell Fischer, "The Computer Revolution Comes to East Asian Collections," *Wilson Library Bulletin* 58 (February 1984), pp. 398–405.

Conjuring in the Academic Library:
The Illusion of Access

Carolyn Bucknall

A frequency count of words in the titles of library science pub--
lications since, say, 1980 would surely identify "access," along
with "information" and perhaps "networks," as among the profession's most repeated words. "Access" has become an annoying word,
and while overuse has contributed to this annoyance, the fault
lies mainly in its essential elusiveness.

Conceptually "accessing" deals with relationships which are
capable of shifting according to one's choice of definition. If A
equals the scholar and B equals the book he is accessing, A can
variously be described as entertaining the possibility of reaching
B, pursuing B through a conduit or connection, nearing B, entering
the threshold of attaining B, or even finally obtaining B. Yet for
all its ambiguity academic librarians have frequently employed
the word with more specificity than was justifiable. It came to me
that we might have chosen it with especial care to explain to faculty
why, with budget cutbacks and all, we actually have this book
available from some point in space and time, but at this particular
moment -- now – at this particular place – here – the book is not
available. In other words, we have "access' to the book.

Is access real or illusionary? When we talk about access, are
we conjuring with words? And if we are, who are we fooling?

In order to consider access in specific contexts it may be useful
first to develop a generalized library model of the process of information delivery and communication.

We can begin with two components essential to the information
process: that which is sought and the seeker. Only in the linking
of the two can information be obtained and inducted. Does information exist if no one can use it? It may be *forgotten* information
or *potential* information, but in truth it is not information until
it informs, until the final communication link with the seeker/
receptor is set in place.

The librarian wishes to facilitate this linkage between the seeker
and his information objectives as effectively as possible. To this

end, the librarian has analyzed most information acquired according to subject, author, title, unique identifying number, etc. The resulting access tools are catalogs and indexes -- in card, hardcopy, microform, electronic and other formats. When the seeker identifies the information sought by reference to the points of analysis in the tools consulted, bibliographical access has taken place. Please note that by this means the seeker has obtained not only the address of the desired information at this point, and *not* the information itself.

If the information sought has been acquired by the library being consulted, the chances for completing the communication chain are pretty good. Assuming that the information is in traditional formats and is not being consulted by another seeker, is not lost, misplaced, out to the bindery, mutilated, embrittled, crumbling, or the victim of a thousand other ills library materials are heir to, actual physical access to information can occur.

On the other hand, the seeker may well have discovered that the information he pursues is in a remote location. Distance is traditionally the greatest impediment to achieving a timely information connection. And while distances are increasingly demolished by the instantaneous character of electronic information flow -- especially as magnified in tandem with other media - geography remains an important consideration in information accessibility.

The seeker, for this part, must be willing and able (literate) to receive the information ultimately obtained. And of course he must be able to distinguish between true and false information, assimilating or rejecting according to his own best judgement. This may be termed intellectual access. It is part of the process of creating knowledge out of information.

In looking at our model for the process of information delivery and communication, we have identified bibliographical access, physical access and intellectual access. It is with physical access that this paper is primarily concerned. For physical access the essential question is: "Can I obtain it here now?" And if I cannot, "How long will it take to get it here?"

For years the central idea in collection building in large research libraries was to acquire as much as possible *here* so that if anyone wanted to see it, it could be obtained *now*. That seemed to have worked for the great research libraries. However, in the seventies external factors of increased publishing and decreased purchasing power forced libraries to reconsider this approach. Ultimately, attempts to build individual libraries of record - that is, libraries having exhaustive representation in every subject collected -- were seen as expensive, anachronistic and doomed to futility.

Given that no single academic library can afford to acquire

all publications for all potential users and uses that might ever exist, what can it reasonably be expected to provide? A bill of rights to access in academic libraries might stipulate that library materials be acquired:

-- in all subjects taught
-- in all suitable media
-- in enough copies
-- in a collecting depth commensurate with the degree offered
-- with due regard for intellectual freedom
                          but
-- as conditioned by the goals of the institution
-- within the constraints of economic resources
-- with reasonable care for the security of the material
-- as permitted by preservation concerns
-- as limited by copyright and other legal considerations

The bill adds up to five pluses and five minuses, five points in support of adequate access and five points constituting obstacles to access.

Acquiring in all subjects taught means selective acquisitions by subject. We are back to the concept of core collections, the need to identify and collect that core of vital materials that will answer a preponderance of the users' print--based library needs. Acquiring all suitable media adds to traditional print--based materials such nonconventional formats as sound recordings, video, film, art slides and fiche, and a variety of electronic media. Selectivity is essential here also. The need for providing single titles in enough copies is so obvious that embellishment to the proposition seems impossible. Yet let it be observed that inadequacy in this respect is a perennial academic library problem. Especially in larger libraries where collection developers may be more removed from circulation information, accurate feedback mechanisms are essential to accom--plish this rather simple objective.

In--depth collecting commensurate with the degree offered provides onsite a great deal, but not all, of the materials needed for graduate and faculty study and research. Even in large research libraries the ideal of resource sharing has been substituted for the ideal of building a stand--alone library of record. Finally, due regard for intellectual freedom implies, within subject limitations, access to materials containing a variety of viewpoints, including those of minorities.

Access to nonconventional resources is frequently shaky and sometimes nonexistent. For example, it is understood that our bill of rights to access applies to microfilms as well as books and journals, and to slides and to video tapes. But does it also apply to manuscripts? To rare books? To computer databases? How about software and microcomputers and playback equipment?

In special collections which concentrate on archives and rare books, physical access to materials is most often strictly regulated. Frequently, scholarly credentials such as letters of introduction from impeccable references are requisite to admittance. Some few collections do profess accessibility to undergraduates, but in practice the undergraduate is most often routinely discouraged. An elitist aura effectively holds this would be scholar at bay, in psychological remove.

Excellent reasons justify this intended snub, first among which are security and preservation. In any library collection security and preservation considerations must be balanced against users' rights to access. In totally open stack undergraduate libraries access is given most weight; in special collections least. A few other maxims are here appropriate. The fewer the users, the greater the security. The fewer the users, the fewer the staff required to service their requests. Undergraduates don't know how to identify and request archives useful to their purposes. Undergraduates don't know how to handle rare books. Undergraduates don't have true research needs; their unnecessary handling of materials, even when correct, merely serves to hasten the deterioration of rare items.

Now somewhere in the middle of the preceding a big line should be drawn to separate the excellent reasons from those that are merely true. The central question that each library must answer for itself is whether there is merit in permitting undergraduates access to rare and archival research materials. Those who decide to pursue the idea further have usually opted for limited, even indirect access. Upper division students are the obvious population target, particularly those enrolled in small seminars and honors courses. Here the agent for effecting the library connection must be a faculty member who is knowledgeable about the collection, its access tools and policies. Student involvement with special materials at the class level may be as elementary as holding a beautiful book or inspecting a variety of bindings or manuscript leaves. Mylar folders and occasional white cotton gloves are the only essential equipment. The key to success in such hands-on sessions is, as in most library focussed education, a function of adequate collaborative preparation on the part of the professor and the librarian.

The subjects in which students might derive benefits are limited only by the collection itself. To seniors in American Studies, for example, historical archives can offer for an honors paper thrilling possibilities that can alter career objectives. That paper could be the first step in the making of an archivist. Our profession has always needed intelligent subject specialists, and access to special collections is one way to attract interested future scholars.

Of course public institutions have far less latitude for limiting access than do private schools, for ultimately a public institution exists for the benefit of the citizenry of that political entity. In some special collections community outreach is a goal. This is especially true when resources for the study of a minority segment of the community, such as Mexican Americans, are the focus of the collection. Some outreach programs generated in this spirit have involved the use of archival materials by public school teachers and, in some cases, even elementary school students.

As to the future of special collections, a few observations may be made. Although, according to Charles Osburn[1] and others, traditional primary materials are yielding to numerical data even, for example, in historical research, special collections will continue to function as research resources for the forseeable future. Aging paper and the deterioration of other materials, as well, have led to the recognition of pressing preservation concerns. For manuscripts particularly we will be determining that access to a facsimile and not the artefact itself is quite satisfactory for most scholarly purposes.

With the developing technologies of optical digital disks for written records and analog video disks for images, problems of preservation, storage space, and physical access may be solved at one brilliant stroke. Reappraisals currently underway regarding the desirability of a simpler approach to the cataloging of manuscripts and archival collections are tremendously encouraging in their promotion of reader bibliographic access, as is the move to place these records with the bibliographic utilities.

On the other hand, donor restrictions will continue to hinder access to some collections and, in public institutions, may actually conflict with public record laws. In this age of lost legal innocence literary and artistic copyright also reduce total access. Moreover, the special collection itself through considerations of prestige may not permit reproductions of its documents to travel outside the library.

In summary the access score for special collections is more negative than positive, but for generally good reasons. However, the trend is toward increasing physical access through new preservation technologies, and more bibliographical access as a result of cataloging simplification and its inclusion in online data base. Some academic libraries are encouraging nontraditional researchers to use their special collections, and are sometimes motivated by enlightened self interest. Legal restrictions seem more present.

To travel from special collections to the world of contemporary media requires some mental adjustment. For archives and rare books collections tend to encourage traditional scholarship and preserve the archaic; they possess a museum--like quality. Media, on the other hand, are associated with lights and movement, sensory participation in global events, the future.

We live in a mediated environment. The television child appre--hends the total context of the visual in a way, perhaps, that the literate, linear, over--the--hill generation may not fully appreciate. But the perception of all of us have been sharpened, yes extended, by a growing array of increasingly sophisticated media. In scholarly works and in student texts, word pictures have been supplanted by real pictures. Media have been trucked or wired into the class--room. In one university, for example, Hollywood movies are used in a classics course to illustrate fact and fiction on life in ancient Rome. Elsewhere, personal computers are provided for all incoming freshmen.

Where will it end? Some of us are worried. Will the computer replace the book?

In 1979 media consciousness had permeated the profession to the point that the Joint ARL/ACRL "Standards for University Libraries" included a pro--media standard.[2] Yet, whether access to media should be a matter of real library commitment is still a matter for debate in many quarters. It is expensive to provide access to appropriate media, well maintained playback equipment, viewing space, and technical support, to say nothing of possible production capacity. Short of miraculous intervention media access in the degree recommended by the standards will be achieved, campus by campus, only through reallocation of funds. If this reallocation must occur within the library budget, the "materials" line is most likely to be tapped, though present equipment and staff lines might also be considered as potential sources.

At one end of the academic media--use scale is the two--year college library; at the other extremity, the research library. It is no coincidence that two--year colleges, unencumbered by self--referring tradition, have felt free to buy whatever was useful, giving no special priority, real or implied, to print--based materials. This has not been possible for large university libraries which by virtue of their size and complexity, are inherently conservative. For in--stance, university library administrators were long constrained to press for ever larger numbers of volumes to add to their collec--tions and subsequently report in annual statistics. Many are still strongly encouraged to beat last year's record, a quantitative per--spective that is difficult to dislodge. Additionally, dedicated alle--giance of longstanding constituencies tends to impede reallocation of funding, as in a shift away from support for books. Moreover, since collecting levels for books and other traditional materials have already been significantly eroded through reduced buying power, these constituencies naturally enough see in media a threat to historic cultural values.

Altogether, library commitment to media generally is not nearly so strong as that for conventional materials, ARL/ACRL standards notwithstanding. Indeed, a media resistance based on economic, political and other grounds, still prevails in many academic institu-tions six years later.

Interestingly, media in support of the visual arts have never encountered much resistance in academia, faculty and students apparently having recognized the necessity for expanded visual references. Photography created the first genuine museum without walls, and other reproduction media -- films, slides and video -- have multiplied its exhibitions. Through access to these media the viewer has become an art center to which art works travel. Reproductions also have other advantages which their originals do not possess. For they are in a form which can be easily manipu-lated. The London *Virgin of the Rocks* can be placed beside the Paris *Virgin* for convenient comparison. More significant for the creative artist, the head of the Mona Lisa can be superimposed on the body of the Sphinx, the Winged Nike of Samothrace made to soar over Cape Canaveral, and Peter Rabbit to compare tummies with the Lascaux Venus. In the fine arts, media have become pri-mary agents of inter-cultural transfer. Technically, with the excep-tion of photocopies, reproduction methods and viewing equipment have achieved reasonable image clarity and color fidelity. Slides, microforms and compact disks successively have demonstrated the storage advantages of the miniaturized image.

Accessibility to some formats of art in reproduction such as microforms, slides or video formats, is limited only by equipment availability. Yet this is a very large proviso, since equipment en-velops the provision not only of hardware, but also of maintenance, repair, viewing space, and operating instruction or operator. Another disadvantage occurs when inadequate indexing to a microform project renders physical access to a very expensive acquisition virtually useless.

However, the great drawback to art in reproduction is that the medium can substantially change the image it carries. Thus a photographic bird's eye view of St. Peter's is not at all the same kind of access as that on actually viewing St. Peter's and entering it on foot. Something was added, but something was lost. In repro-duction we lose the environment – geographical, historical and cul-tural – in which the object is normally located. Our personal rela-tionship to the object is altered, including a reference to scale, and there is some loss of texture and depth.

Recognizing that art in reproduction is something less (and something more) than the original in no way diminishes its usefulness. Within budget limitations academic libraries appear to have been quite responsive to needs for media access in the study of the visual arts.

A more problematic media subset, electronic media, has been with us for many fewer years. But in that time profound changes for libraries have been set in motion. Electronically based information on the library itself has been most thoroughly developed. Data relating to the bibliographic description, the location, and availability of materials in our collections has been created, stored and made accessible. By means of networking much of this is shared with other libraries and through electronic mail interlibrary loan requests are relayed.

Commercially constructed and maintained databases -- numeric, bibliographic and textual -- have also been made accessible through libraries and other information brokers. Just at the point where libraries were comfortable with manipulating data tapes, and making free database searches for ready reference purposes, new challenges in the form of microcomputers exploded on the scene. Demand for library acquisition of public use microcomputers, commercial software, and manuals quickly followed and will no doubt continue to grow. Moreover, appeals for the provision of storage and access to locally generated software have also been addressed to libraries. Responses have repeated patterns observed with other media, generally; among academic libraries two--year colleges and other smaller schools are in the vanguard. The larger issues of institutional policy and funding as well as the procedural problems of circulation, maintenance and copyright must all be carefully considered and collection development policies established. Basically these are the same concerns identified in dealing with other media, but for each format the resolution is different.

Where are libraries now in regard to access to electronic media? In all candor, not very far. While there are stellar performances in finite areas, such as online catalogs or library microcomputer centers, no single library has been able to advance at a consistent pace across the breadth of the electronic frontier. And one of the gravest of issues, cost--recovery fees for access to commercial databases, has not been laid to rest by anyone. Generally speaking, electronic information about the library itself is still incomplete but access is open, while access to most other types of databases must be purchased. Very few academic libraries have provided adequate access, and most have provided no access at all, to micro--computers and their software.

Full text databases produced to date have been designed to test the market. Essentially they are to determine whether the desire for instantaneous viewing or overnight transmission of journal articles, for example, coincides with willingness to pay for the cost of the service. Journals which have elected to publish exclusively online or dually online and on paper also are a part of this enlarging textual electronic databank.

F. Wilfrid Lancaster sized up the situation in 1978 and predicted:

> Whether we like it or not, society is evolving from one whose formal communication has, for centuries, been based almost exclusively on print on paper to one whose formal communication will be largely paperless (i.e. electronic).[3]

However, the adaptability of online publishing for a full range of information purposes is not yet proved. In the future electronic publishing could also be distributed offline by means of optical or possibly video disks. In the same vein currently online data files could be distributed as disks to libraries or the end user. Some of us have been thinking of the library of the future as a paperless electronic switching center. But perhaps it will still collect material objects to which physical access will still be demanded, only computer disks will have been substituted for books. More likely it could be a combination of the two, that is, a switching center plus a collection of physical objects (disks and more traditional formats) which can be directed to the end user at remote locations, through cable television or other media.

In a recent newsletter John Dessauer, of the Book Industry Study Group, traces the development of the current "cultural revolution" and foresees continued expansion of the book reading boom begun in post World War II years.[4] My personal opinion is that information available electronically will continue to burgeon, but that it will not overthrow and supplant the printed word. On the contrary the two will persist in amity, each adapting to the purposes for which it is uniquely suited. Their relationship parallels that of art and photography. Despite very gloomy predictions, art not only survived photography's challenge but actually seemed to wax in the onslaught. When art turned to abstraction, some interpreted that movement as a reaction to losing portraiture to photography. Now that figural paintings are once more fashionable and abstraction a frequent interest of photography, we can cheerfully admit that a great deal of cause and effect resides chiefly in the minds of men. Paintings and photographs are not at all in conflict. They are different. And each is exploited so as best to realize its unique characteristics.

Issues of access, particularly to the traditional formats of books and journals, have been enormously conditioned by resource sharing, especially as enhanced by networking. Despite the wonders of the electronic world, resource sharing still ideally takes place among institutions in geographical proximity, so that document delivery time or user travel time is minimized. Participants also need to be proximate in their levels of development, each with different specialties or emphases it is committed to maintain in its own best interests. And each needs to have formulated a collection develop-ment policy that uses shared and mutually understood language. Protocols must be in place on responsibilities for the acquisition of expensive items, interlibrary loan costs, net lender status, docu-ment delivery, etc. And while some type of shared bibliographic access is necessary, shared bibliographic access via electronic net-working is most helpful.

The foregoing is the orthodox view of resource sharing freely adapted from "A Guide to Coordinated and Cooperative Collection Development," published by the Resources and Technical Services Division of the American Library Association in 1983.[5] As I have stated in the case, it applies best to the local or regional level. How-ever, with some elaboration, such as the addition of primary collect-ing, cataloging, and preservation responsibilities by subject, the guidelines can be made to refer to a resource sharing plan of national scope. In fact, the National Collections Inventory Project, under the auspices of the Association of Research Libraries, is expanding on the influential model for distributed collection development and management originally developed by the Research Libraries Group (RLG). In this project the RLG conspectus is being applied to other research library collections. An anticipated product of all this effort is a distributed national library of record composed of those subject elements of research libraries that have achieved unusual strength nationwide.

I mention this project particularly because I see in it a possible solution to costly redundancies in books amassed and warehoused, not for now, but for the future. There is an obvious reallocation potential for savings thus effected. Of greater consequence is the fact that the project's method was conceived in an online environ-ment and will ultimately be implemented through networking. Meanwhile, the advent of an online interlibrary loan system through another bibliographic utility, OCLC, has also fostered a network of reciprocity. These activities are sustaining intense participant interaction.

We are here witnessing a potent phenomenon. A high degree of institutional interaction, ostensibly impersonal, has generated a quickened sense of involvement to those individuals having a role in the process. The human appeal of electronic networking is dramatic and direct, releasing prodigious individual energy.

Perhaps a contributing factor is the present ubiquity of informa-tion; it is no longer a rarefied commodity. Another factor may be the weakening of old hierarchical structures. Computers are great democratizers. Instead of the prewar summitry of a handful of library educators or the somewhat distanced leadership of the great academic library directors of that more leisurely era, librarians at every level are talking together. Conversations generated because of the medium take place online, in user groups, in formal convo-cations and in casual encounters. We have been driven to learning to talk with each other – to great advantage. Our computers are talking with each other, too. Our bibliographic utilities have opened a dialog. We are interested in all manner of national and interna-tional standards to facilitate these dialogs, these interactions.

We have ended our splendid isolation, each separate from the other. This new access – the intellectual, interpersonal access to other librarians may well be the great legacy of computer networking to the library profession. As a dynamic it can effect far–reaching and as yet unanticipated consequences. In the words of Marshall McLuhan:

> Nobody yet knows the languages inherent in the new techno-logical culture; we are all technological idiots in terms of the new situation. Our most impressive words and thoughts betray us by referring to the previously existent, not to the present.[6]

NOTES

1. Charles B. Osburn, *Academic Research and Library Resources: Changing Patterns in America,* New Directions in Librarianship, no. 3 (Westport, Conn.: Greenwood Press, 1979), 148.

2. "Standards for University Libraries," *College & Research Libra-ries News,* April 1979, 101–110.

3. F. Wilfrid Lancaster, "Whither Libraries, or Wither Libraries," *College and Research Libraries* 40 (September 1978): 346.

4. John P. Dessauer, "The Cultural Revolution," *Book Industry Study Group Trends Update* 3 (August 1984): 1–4.

5. Paul H. Mosher and Marcia Pankake, "A Guide to Coordinated and Cooperative Collection Development," *Library Resources and Technical Services* 27 (October/December): 417–431.

6. Marshall McLuhan, *Counterblast* (New York: Harcourt, Brace & World, 1969), 16.

Reduction In Access And Rights

Donald E. Riggs

"Only one thing is impossible for God: to find any sense in any copyright law on the planet."   –Mark Twain

Since the implementation of the new copyright law in 1978, librarians have made contradictory observations on the impact of the new law on access to scholarly information. For example, some librarians have observed that the new law has had little or no effect on their library users, while others have stated quite the contrary. Nonetheless, it is the opinion of this writer that the new copyright law has not enhanced access to and utilization of scholarly resources. A case for this opinion is given in the following paragraphs.

The word "copyright" has essentially two meanings: the right to copy and the right to control. It can be traced back to the early Renaissance when the first exclusive rights were granted to one's literary creations and inventions. Johann Gutenberg's invention of the printing press started an explosion in writing and diffusing a knowledge of the civilization. His movable type also brought forth some of the first disputes and litigations involving "copy-righted" materials. England's Queen Anne established the precedent for most of the copyright laws now in existence by her 1710 Statute on Copyright. The Statute clarified the author's entitlement to ownership rights and it set forth the rights regarding the use and sale of literary property.

Noah Webster was instrumental in getting the United States to create its first copyright law in 1790. To prevent piracy of his popular *The American Spelling Book,* Webster lobbied for copyright and was effective in getting laws passed in six states. Fourteen years after gaining independence, the United States Congress enacted its first law on copyright in May 1790. The law provided protection for books, maps and charts for 14 years with the understanding that a renewal for another 14 years was possible. On October 19, 1976, President Gerald R. Ford signed Public Law 94–553, General

Revision of the Copyright Law. The new law became effective January 1, 1978, and it marked the first time since 1909 that the United States had a new copyright law.

The House Committee report accompanying P.L. 94–553 gives the following background as justification for replacing the 1909 copyright law:

> Since that time significant changes in technology have affected the operation of the copyright law. Motion pictures and sound recordings had just made their appearance in 1909, and radio and television were still in the early stages of their development. During the past half century a wide range of new techniques for capturing and communicating printed matter, visual images, and recorded sounds have come into use, and the increasing use of information, storage and retrieval devices, communications satellites, and laser technology promises even greater changes in the near future. The technical advances have generated new industries and new methods for the reproduction and dissemination of copyrighted works, and the business relations between authors and users have evolved new patterns.[1]

Significant Changes

> "Copyrighting as a monopolistic practice can only be justified to the extent it serves the public good. That is why the Constitution insists that it be secured only for limited times."
> --Massachusetts Congressman Robert F. Drinan

The American Library Association delineated the highlights of the new copyright law:

- Copyright duration is extended to the life of the author plus 50 years. When the new law became effective in January 1978, existing copyrights under the old system were extended to span a total term of 75 years, automatically in the case of copyrights already renewed for a second term, but only if renewed in the case of first--term copyrights.

-- Fair use doctrine is given statutory recognition for the first time.

-- Federal copyright law is extended to unpublished works.

-- The old system of common law copyright is pre--empted. The new copyright law pre--empts and abolishes any right under state common or statutory law that comes within the scope of the federal copyright law (except for rights in pre--1972 sound recordings which are covered by state statute or common law until 2047).

-- Copyright liability is extended to two previously exempted groups -- cable television systems, and the operators of juke--boxes. Both will be entitled to compulsory licenses.

-- A Copyright Royalty Tribunal is to review royalty rates and settle disputes among parties entitled to several specified types of statutory royalties (in areas not directly affecting libraries).

-- An American Television and Radio Archive is to be established in the Library of Congress.[2]

Economic Myths

"If any person has a social responsibility, it is the publisher of books. For we face the loss of communications and an acute absence of ideas in almost every other medium, the princi--pal culprit being concentration and lust for the dollar. Yours is a health industry . . . but earning reports are the siren song of concentration. An industry has the capability of monitoring its own trends and to warn against what may be attractive to the accountants, but may be bitter to society."
—Arizona Congressman Morris K. Udall

Unquestionably, the 1909 copyright law had to be replaced. Many changes, especially technological ones, stipulated that the law be made current. Property rights of the copyright holder had to be made more specific. Nevertheless, Congressman Udall's mes--sage is noteworthy. Society does not want to deny the rights of authors. However, society does want to ensure that access to infor--mation is available. This right has to be guaranteed to our citizenry.

Section 108 of Public Law 94--553 is indeed evidence of progress toward achieving the intended balance between the rights of creators and access rights of users to copyrighted works. The Association of American Publishers (AAP) does not believe the new copyright law is working; it is advocating stiffer penalties for violations of the law. AAP contends that the publishers are still losing large sums of money annually due to the huge number of illegal photo--copies being made. The absence of economic harm must be assured the copyright owners while concurrently assuring the citizenry access to scholarly information. The history of copyright has been

73

one of changing views of society as to where the line should be drawn between the rights of the individual and the interests of the general public.

King Research, Inc., prepared a report for the U.S. Copyright Office entitled *Libraries, Publishers, and Photocopying*. Some of the findings reflected in the report included:

A. Libraries participating in the study indicated they had increased expenditures for serials by 43 percent in current dollars, or 12 percent in constant dollars, between 1976 and 1980.

B. A decrease of 16 percent in library staff photocopying of all types of materials occurred between 1976 and 1981.

C. Sixty--nine percent of all photocopying transactions involved the making of only one copy; 76 percent of all serial photo-copying transactions involved the making of only one copy.

D. Only 21 percent of 61 million interlibrary loan requests were filled with photocopies.

E. Publishers' revenues increased significantly from 1976 to 1980.[3]

The above findings clearly indicate that the publishers' worries about photocopying were unsubstantiated. Wholesale photocopying did not occur. Further perplexing the situation, AAP is now de--manding that the copyright law be amended again. AAP believes that the volume of photocopying reported by King Research is underestimated. It also contends that large amounts of illegal photocopying takes place on library controlled machines. While on the other hand, the American Library Association (ALA) believes that libraries have overwhelmingly complied with the new copyright law.

The large profits that may have been expected by some pub-lishers were not realized by implementing stricter copyright regu-lations. Publishers' revenues have increased, but not significantly. Unfounded fears about libraries and their use of copyrighted mater-ials have caused counterproductive irritations between librarians and publishers.

Fair Use

"Our copyright laws . . . impose hardships upon the copyright proprietor which are not essential to the fair practices of the public; they are difficult for the courts to interpret and impos--

74

sible for the Copyright Office to administer to the satisfaction of the public." Theodore Roosevelt

The doctrine of "fair use" is given statutory recognition in P.L. 94553. From the library user's stance, fair use is a doctrine that assures equity and fairness in the access to information. Much of the new law's interpretation leans toward the exclusivity and rights of copyright holders. Section 107, offering more flexibility, reads as follows:

Limitations on exclusive rights: fair use.

Notwithstanding the provisions of section 106, the fair use of a copyrighted work, including such use by reproduction in copies of phonorecords or by any other means specified by that section, for purposes such as criticism, comment, news reporting, teaching (including multiple copies for classroom use), scholarship, or research, is not an infringement of copyright. In determining whether the use made of a work in any particular case is a fair use, the factors to be considered shall include:

(1) The purpose and character of the user, including whether such use is of a commercial nature or is for nonprofit educational purposes;

(2) The nature of the copyrighted work;

(3) The amount and substantiality of the portion used in relation to the copyrighted work as a whole; and

(4) The effect of the use upon the potential market for or value of the copyrighted work.[4]

The foregoing four factors seem to provide considerable freedom to educational photocopiers; however, the language is rather vague and will stimulate some interesting interpretations in the courts. Copyright owners have expressed many fears about the potential of the fair use doctrine seriously undercutting their sales. The new law does not give the principle of fair use unrestricted support since the courts remain free to interpret the doctrine in accordance with rapid technological changes and the merits of each case. There does not appear to be any one satisfactory and generally accepted definition of fair use upon which the courts have agreed. "Good faith and fair dealing" are necessary ingredients for an effective fair use doctrine. "Good faith" is not mentioned in the new law, but it may be the most important factor of all. Many of the questions of ambiguity cause anxieties on the part of librarians.

The fair use doctrine has assisted libraries in the dissemination of information. Prior to the 1978 copyright law, fair use was a nebulous issue. Librarians remain unclear on the precise interpretation of fair use, but they now have a document on which they can base their arguments for photocopying materials and placing items on reserve. Vagueness still exists on the application of fair use to databases and computer programs.

The library user has benefited from the enactment of fair use in various ways. According to the law, the user of the library materials can reasonably use another person's creative works if there is no economic harm done to the copyright owner. Naturally, plagiarism would be determined as an unfair use of another's creation.

If the publishers succeed in admending the 1978 copyright law, Section 107 (fair use) will likely undergo the greatest revision. Publishing houses have expressed great concern about the impact of "fair use" on their livelihoods. Publishers are expected to promote their subsistence and academic librarians are charged with making available scholarly information to the extent permitted by law. Students and faculty should be expected to comply fully with the fair use standards. In summary, they should be aware of four fair use factors: (1) The legal amount (e.g., 10 lines of poetry) of a copyrighted work they can use, (2) The type (e.g., an index) of copyrighted work they can use without obtaining permission, (3) For what purposes they can use the work (e.g., scholarship versus for-profit intent), and (4) Will the use of the material cause financial harm to the copyrighted work?

Photocopying

"Photocopying of entire books is both illegal and inane."
–Jay K. Lucker

The photocopier has been perceived by some as the greatest threat to the survival of the publishing industry. The bulk of the fears by publishing houses centers around photocopying practices. Some publishers have gone as far to say that photocopiers are destroying them. And they are attempting to counteract their perceived devastation in various ways. For example, some publishers have thrown a "chilling effect" on the photocopying and use of materials by placing the following statement in their books: "No part of this publication may be reproduced or transmitted in any form

76

or by any means, electronic or mechanical, including photocopying, recording, or by any information storage and retrieval system, without permission in writing from ―――――――――." This statement is an example of reduction in access to materials and in curtailment of the rights of users. It also runs counter to specific parts of Sections 107 and 108 of P.L. 94–553. Librarians and teachers, for example, are specifically allowed by the fair use section of the copy right law to photocopy parts of books. Nevertheless, such language appearing in the statement intimidates them and possibly will refrain them from photocopying from a book bearing the statement, regardless of their right to do so.

An attempt to determine the extent of photocopying was made by King Research, Inc., in 1980 and 1981.[5] The survey included users, publishers, and libraries (all types except school libraries). One interesting conclusion of the survey was that academic libraries were more faithful in adhering to the copyright guidelines than any other type of library. Needless to say, most of the nation's scholarly information is found in our academic libraries. Academic libraries refused to fill interlibrary loan requests that violated copyright interpretations more than any other type of library.

The report indicated that 600–million copies are made on photocopying machines in libraries each year. The report re–inforced the publishers fears that several copies were being made on uncontrolled copies outside of the libraries. Approximately one–half of the libraries surveyed reported that there was a photocopy machine found within walking distance of the library.

Of the 823 library users interviewed (as they were making copies) during the King study, fewer than 56% were copying library materials. Of this number, 66% were making only one copy. And about 41% of these users described their apprehension of the copyright regulations to be best summarized by the statement "could copy if used for educational or research purposes."

Another 1,157 users were interviewed as they entered 21 different types of libraries in five cities. The report mentions that more than half of those users interviewed stated that the last copy made or obtained was between one and five pages long. Only 1.8% of the users reported that they had requested a library to make a copy for them and was refused.

When asked what type of copies they last made, over 24% of the users stated they copied less than a chapter from a book. However, about 14% indicated that they had copied one or more chapters. The largest amount of this type of copying occurred in academic libraries.

Slightly over 29% of those interviewed said they had photocopied all or parts of books on one to three occasions within the past six months. Twenty--four percent had not photocopied any at all, less than 19% four to six times, and more than 26% claimed more than six times. Special non--profit libraries did the largest percentage of photocopying of books.

It is interesting to note that the reports divulge there was an overall decline of 16% in the number of copies made of serials, books and other materials between 1976 and 1981. However, the bulk of the decline occurred in photocopying of serials. Photo--copying of books actually increased by 2%.

King Research also sent questionnaires to publishers regarding the number of requests they had received for permission to photo--copy works. It was discovered that more requests were received to photocopy books or book chapters (84,700 requests) than serials or serial articles (78,800 requests). There was an insignificant difference in the number of requests received when compared with the number received in a similar study done in 1976. More than 60% of the publishers said they granted the requests in full. Most of them stated that they did not ask for any monetary reward for granting permission to photocopy.

About half of all photocopying done on machines in libraries are for items brought in from outside of the libraries. Nevertheless, publishers continue to argue that photocopying practices do them financial harm, and librarians believe the publishers are overestimat--ing the amount of photocopying done by users.

Section 108 of the 1978 copyright law addresses the issue of reproduction/copying by libraries and archives.[6] Copying that relates to fair use falls under Section 107, but some types of library copying which may not be fair use are authorized by Section 108. However, it should be understood that the specific types of library photocopying authorized in Section 108 does not limit the library's fair use right.

General conditions and limitations of copying authorized in Section 108 include the following:

1. The copy is made without any purpose of direct or indirect commercial advantage.

2. The collections of the library are open to the public or available not only to researchers affiliated with the library, but also to other persons doing research in a specified field.

3. The copy includes a notice of copyright.

Charles Martell summarized the "may's" and "may not's" of the new copy regulations as follows:

A teacher MAY NOT and by extension a library for a teacher (where applicable) MAY NOT:

1. Make multiple copies of a work for classroom use if it has already been copied for another class in the same institution.

2. Make multiple copies of a short poem, article, story, or essay from the same author more than once in a class term or make multiple copies from the same collective work or periodical issue more than three times a term.

3. Make multiple copies of works more than nine times in the same class term.

4. Make multiple copies long in advance of the actual use of those copies.

5. Make multiple copies at the suggestion or direction of another individual.

6. Make multiple copies for distribution that do not contain (individually) a notice of copyright.

7. Make a copy or copies that imply or attribute an ownership position to the library.

8. Make copies for private reserve files, departmental reserve collections, or general library units if the cumulative effect exceeds the Guidelines in the same class term.

9. Make a single copy or multiple copies of any item for use from term to term.

10. Make a copy of works to take the place of an anthology.

11. Make a copy (copies) for charge in excess of costs.

12. Direct students to make photocopies from either an original item or a photocopy of that item for any course.

13. Make a copy of "consumable" materials, such as workbooks.

A teacher MAY:

1. Make a single copy for use in scholarly research, or in teaching,

79

or in preparation for teaching a class of the following:

- A chapter from a book.

-- An article from a periodical or newspaper.

- A short story, short essay, or short poem, whether or not from a collected work.

-- A chart, graph, diagram, drawing, cartoon, or picture from a book, periodical, or newspaper.

2. Make multiple copies for classroom use only and not to exceed one per student in a class of the following:

-- A complete poem, if it is less than 250 words and printed on not more than two pages.

- An excerpt from a longer poem, if it is less than 2,500 words.

-- An excerpt from a prose work, if it is less than 1,000 words or 10 percent of the work, whichever is less.

-- One chart, graph, diagram, drawing, cartoon, or picture per book or periodical.

A library MAY NOT:

1. Make (distribute) any copy of material that does not contain a notice of copyright.

2. Make a single copy of more than a single article from any one issue of a journal (except for a teacher in classroom situations).

A library MAY:

1. Make copies of unpublished works for purposes of preservation and security.

2. Make copies of published works for purposes or replacement of damaged copies.

3. Make (request) copies of copyrighted material in extension of the restrictions noted above if it owns the material but cannot provide access to it at the time.[7]

The foregoing guidelines/regulations need to be supported by local guidelines. After all is said and done, libraries remain legally obligated to adhere to the federal law. Care has to be taken to avoid unreasonable and excessive photocopying. It is one thing to photocopy in the good faith belief that is legal under the statutes, but it is quite another to insist upon photocopying which totally disregards the rights of the copyright holder.

The library community must work together in abiding by the interpretation of P.L. 94–553. It would be a serious blow to the current practices of accessing scholarly information, for example, if educational photocopying in general were to be placed under any stricter federal regulations.

Without doubt, Section 108 has provided clarification on what can and cannot be photocopied. At the same time, it has created some obstacles in the pursuit of scholarship and learning. Fair use becomes a larger issue in the provision of access to scholarly resources in the event that photocopying regulations do become more restrictive.

Copyright owners fear reserve practices in academic libraries are undercutting the sale of their work. This would be true if entire books or a significant part thereof are photocopied. In most cases, before a significant part of a book is photocopied, a library would likely purchase that book. Librarians have been using good judgment as to reasonable limits pertaining to the length of works photo-copied for reserve. Any efforts to further restrict what academic libraries can photocopy for reserve will undoubtedly impede the learning process and will run counter to fair use interpretations.

Exclusive rights in copyrighted works must never be interpreted by law as meaning that academic libraries shall not place photo-copied materials on reserve. An interpretation of this nature would run diametrically opposed to any efforts of exercising fair use in educational settings.

Access Limitations to Various Materials

"We cannot and will not put up with continued stealing by anyone, including those who seek to wrap themselves in the mantle of so--called nonprofit activity."
                    --Leonard Feist, National Music Publishers' Association

Access to various types of scholarly materials is inhibited by the new copyright law. Guidelines attendant to Section 107 do not provide for the needs of music libraries. Also, the concept of music as "entertainment" is strongly reflected in the wording of Section 108 (h) of the current law. The highly restrictive law on copying music materials has caused extreme hardship on users of music libraries. There has been very little progress in alleviating the constraints placed on music libraries by the copyright legislation. Music librarians have essentially discontinued making copies of music materials for reserve.

It is common knowledge that research university libraries have as many unpublished materials as those that have been published and copyrighted in the traditional manner. The 1978 copyright law placed unpublished manuscripts under copyright for the first time. Perpetual common–law copyright for unpublished works ended on January 1, 1978. How does the fair use concept apply to unpublished materials? One can only assume that it applies to these materials in the same manner as regularly copyrighted materials. However, Sections 107 and 108 do not clearly address this issue. At best, one can only deduct that confusion and concern exist about the legal use of unpublished materials. Granted, these valuable historical research materials need copyright protection. However, there are numerous unanswered questions regarding the photocopying of these archival materials. There is definitely a need for further clarification of the law. Until the law is inter-preted more clearly, the apprehension on the part of archivists and curators about how far they can go in giving permission to photocopy the unpublished materials will unquestionably have a negative impact on the use of these materials. Arguing that unpub-lished materials are subsumed under the term "copyrighted work" is not good enough. Confusion regarding the copying of unpublished materials awaits interpretation by the courts.

New Technology

"Will failure to give adequate copyright protection for the reproduction of creative materials on optical discs, computers . . . discourage the creator of the intellectual property?"
　　　　　　　　　　　　–Colorado Congresswoman Patricia Schroeder

The introduction of modern technology in our ever–changing environment brings with it more complexities to the copyright law as it applies to accessing scholarly information. In reality, technology is not new. The printing press and the photocopies are, in a sense, technological developments. Nevertheless, com-pounding the copyright issue, we now are seeking legal interpreta-tions on how the computer, videodisc, satellite broadcasting, non-bibliographic databases, television, audio and video recordings, and laser holography all fit into the "what can or cannot be repro-duced syndrome." The rate of technological change will only intensify and the technology–copyright issues will become more confused. Librarians will never be absolutely sure what they are producing is being done legally. Guidelines on the new technology and copyright will remain only such until they are tried in the courts. The famous "Betamax" case (Universal Studios v. Sony Corporation) is only a harbinger of what will come in litigations. Courts are currently recognizing "fair use" as a pivotal factor in many of the technology–copyright cases. How much longer will the courts recognize that the copyright monopoly in one work cannot be so overarching as to prohibit the public from having access to a second copy of the work? We are indeed living in interesting times and technology has most certainly improved our quality of life. And, yes, technology has created a bewildering situation for all of us whenever we attempt to apply copyright law to it.

Conclusion

To say that the new copyright law greatly enhanced access to scholarly information would be a blatant falsehood. To say that the new copyright regulations are not needed is also false. What one can say with some degree of accuracy is that the 1978 copyright law was required to provide greater protection for the copyright owners, and that the law created some complexities that have not enhanced access to scholarly information. Hidden costs, and some obvious ones, have been imposed on libraries by the new laws.

Whenever prophets claim that the traditional library of today will radically change as a result of electronic publishing, one cannot help to wonder if publishers and other copyright owners of creative works will ever permit such a revolution in our delivery of scholarly information. Without question, the profit motive has been a significant cornerstone in the entire copyright matter. Needless to say, prevention of financial harm is not all wrong. What is wrong with our current copyright system is that copyright owners and librarians have not been able to reach a common ground. Thank goodness for the fair use provision in the 1978 law; otherwise, everything copied by libraries would require some sort of payment to the copyright owner.

In sum, copyright owners and libraries have different philosophical stances. These differences of opinion seriously impact the basic rights of the proprietor and the rights of the user of scholarly information. Our society has belabored long enough with these differences. It is time for all of us to recognize that copyright cannot deny access to information.

REFERENCES

1. *The New Copyright Law: Questions Teachers & Librarians Ask* (Washington, D.C.: National Education Association, 1977), p. 10.

2. *Librarian's Guide to the New Copyright Law* (Chicago: American Library Association, 1977), p. 1.

3. Dennis D. McDonald, et al. *Libraries, Publishers, and Photo-copying: Final Report Surveys Conducted for the United States Copyright Office* (Rockville, MD: King Research Co., 1982).

4. Public Law 94--553, Section 107.

5. McDonald, various pages.

6. Public Law No. 94--553, Section 108.

7. Charles Martell, "Copyright Law and Reserve Operations -- An Interpretation." *College & Research Libraries News* 39 (January 1978): 5--6.

Electronic Publishing
and the
Scholar's Workshop

Robin Downes

Forty years after his last year as an intern in a major New York
hospital, Lewis Thomas wrote of his education in medicine and
the turning point it reached in that year. He described the limitation
of medical practice to diagnosis and prognosis, with the rare excep--
tion in which a pathological state could be altered or -- even more
rarely -- cured. His medical school experience in the 1930's was
little changed from that of his father a generation before. The
year 1937, he wrote, was a landmark in the practice of medicine.
Sulfanilamides were used clinically for the first time, to be followed
in a few years by the tidal wave of chemical therapeutics and medical
technology which we know today as medical science and practice.
Lewis Thomas, who chronicled those events in his book of essays
The Youngest Profession: Notes of a Medicine Watcher, [Thomas,
Lewis. The Youngest Profession: Notes of a Medicine--Watcher.
New York, Viking Press, 1983] wrote of the astonishment of physi--
cians as they gathered at the bedsides of patients who, ill with
any of hundreds of mortal diseases, suddenly and dramatically
were restored to health. Nothing in their experience -- as students,
interns, and physicians -- had prepared them for a profession which
could literally cure sick people.
The revolution in medical education and practice which began
in 1937 transformed the role of the physician, but did not -- ob--
viously -- eliminate it. As the tools of the profession were sharpened,
its practitioners used them to deal proactively instead of passively
with disease. Often the tools were borrowed from other sciences
and applied to medicine, but physicians took control of their appli--
cation to medicine. No longer restricted to diagnosis and prognosis,
physicians thus became active players in the game of living and
dying.
Transferring this historical example to the role of librarians
in supporting research raises questions for librarians in the 1980's
as profound as those faced by physicians in 1937. Deliberately
I have used the term "research librarians" and not "research libra--

ries." As Lancaster has pointed out [Lancaster, F.W. "Implications for Library and Information Science," *Library Trends,* Winter 1984, p. 337--348] the identification of librarians with libraries as institutions has misled their clients as to the true capabilities of the profession. To a lesser degree, it has limited the aggressiveness of librarians in seizing control of the tools they need to take command of their own destinies. Research *libraries* will not adapt to a potential revolution in the publication and use of information, nor did hospitals lead a transformation of medical practice.

In this paper I will discuss the tools which electronic publishing will put into the hands of whoever will claim them. And although I have begun with a hopeful analogy, not everyone is hopeful. Lancaster, again, sees little hope that libraries will survive at all except as museums of the age of paper publishing. In somewhat more hopeful futurist models, Nina Matheson and others see "libraries" as being absorbed into "integrated academic information centers," in which textual and numeric data--bases from many sources and types are stored and used electronically.

Each of these hypothetical models projects two or more stages through which research libraries will pass, from the "traditional" library to the future "integrated academic information center." This last stage is the only one of genuine interest to our discussion, since it represents the revolutionary stage. This futurist model assumes, first, that a major share of the information now acquired by research libraries in paper formats will become available in electronic form. A second assumption is that the library's contribution to an institution--wide academic information center will be bibliographic and full--text, but that it will be only one component of a multi--use campus database. Other components in the database might include in--house clinical records, links to specialized clinical databases maintained by medical centers at locations scattered across the United States, student records, numeric data files, and links to instructional or research--support software packages mounted on the appropriate level of computing. The third assumption is that the university computing environment will consist of one or more local area networks, with widely--distributed access to information stored and disseminated electronically. Some of the library data files in this computer intensive environment would be exclusively local, others would be locally--held copies of national databases, and in other cases, links would be made from the local area networks to data files created and maintained at the national level.

In developing these hypothetical models, the designers have proceeded from the perceived needs of researchers to the specifications of the models. They have, so to speak, hypothesized in 1930 the discovery of antibiotics and swept us onward to the bedsides of patients who are, they assert, being treated by pharmaceutical chemists while physicians have become museum curators. My approach, on the other hand, treats changes in research library models as end products of developments in technology and in the publishing industry. I would predict that, in the worst case, librarians will wait for publishers to design and market new information products, and that librarians will operate in a reactive rather than a proactive mode as these changes occur. In the best case, on the other hand, entreprenurial librarians will find an opportunity to participate actively in the design of new information products. And there is reason for optimism. The truly important progress in research libraries in the last generation has been made by pioneering entrepreneurs who applied computing and telecommunications technology to the bibliographic records and financial and inventory transactions of research libraries.

If librarians -- entrepreneurs or not -- overcome their enchantment with hypothetical constructs, what realistically are the issues to be faced in an expansion of electronic publishing which at the same time meets the needs of scholars and librarians in the academic marketplace? Who, for example, are the principal stakeholders in this evolution to a new stage of publishing and of research library service? Can librarians contribute to this evolution, and help to shape it to the interests of scholars and researchers? To begin, it should be understood that much information is already available in electronic form as a by-product of the printing process. The lack of industry--wide standards has been a crucial obstacle to the creation and competitive pricing of new information products based on this store of electronic data. Why is this so?

The economic benefits of electronic publishing can be fully realized only if the author's keystrokes are captured in standard form at the time the manuscript is keyboarded by the author. Additional coding and formatting of the electronic manuscript for design and marketing of alternative information products could be a joint responsibility of the author, publisher, and possibly the consumer, whether the consumer is an individual, a university, a corporation, or a government agency.

The author's keystrokes then become valuable because the publisher's production systems can economically process input from the scores of vendor--distinctive personal computers, word processors, electronic typewriters and mainframes that authors use for manuscript preparation. A standard will make this possible by replacing with standard coding the unique set of internal codes on which each class of hardware now operates, making it incompatible with equipment of another manufacturer.

Progress is being made on developing such a standard. If it is successfully developed and adopted, it would be possible for the same electronically encoded record to flow with minimal change from author to editor, to publisher, and potentially to the market place. The standards project is co--sponsored by the Association of America Publishers and the Council on Library Resources. An advisory council of major stakeholders includes selected ANSI and ISO representatives, the IEEE, the Printing Industry Association, international and national associations of scientific, medical, and technical publishers, the Author's League, authors and publishers of style manuals, the Modern Languages Association, and many other agencies and professional associations.

A standard is expected in draft form in 1985. If a standard is adopted within 2--3 years after this date, the cost reductions for publishers and the opportunity to widen markets can be expected to cause rapid spread of the technology of electronic manuscript preparation in the publishing industry. The huge amounts of infor--mation now available in paper formats will then become candidates for marketing in electronic form at rates far below the prices now charged for electronic information products. Publishers will be able to market information tailored to the needs of consumers in new and creative ways.

Since the electronic record will be capable of containing ab--stracting and indexing information, the potential exists for selective retrieval of information by sophisticated sets of search keys and consumer--oriented menus. A researcher at a terminal in an office or laboratory could receive citations in his or her discipline, request immediate printout of full or partial text as needed, and assemble packages of textual and non--textual data as needed.

Parenthetically, the same conditions of vendor--specific hardware and publisher specific coding now restrict the potential of the vast computerized databases of citations and abstracts of journal and report literature. Librarians provide access to these databases for researchers, but high costs to consumers restrict the potential market. The lack of an industry standard inflates costs, limits the interchange of electronic data, and inhibits the creative develop--ment of easy--to--use search protocols.

With this in mind, it can be seen that the design of electronic information products for the research library market also requires that bibliographic control in standardized form be added to the electronic manuscript at some stage of the publication process. No longer should it be necessary, or even practical, for cataloging to be created by the consumer. Indexing and abstracting publica--tions, now sold to consumers separately, would be packaged and sold with the full text documents to which they refer. Abstracting

88

and indexing agencies which added coded terms to the electronic manuscripts could also market the coded indexing data separately as an electronic data base or in hard copy, as desired.

The impact of the publisher's ability to broaden the design of information products will eventually be felt by authors as well. As the capacity develops to write and sell a book or journal article as a single "package", or to sell separately any segment or combina-- tion of segments of the package, the concept of writing a published "work" may undergo change. This becomes clear when we recognize that if the separate pieces of a traditional book -- introduction, chapters, appendices, tables, diagrams, and the like -- can be sepa-- rately coded and indexed, they can also be re--assembled, marketed, sold, and used in any form desired by the consumer. A consumer might need the complete package, and acquire it as a standard book. Other consumer products might, on the other hand, be an assembly of articles, chapters, tables, and diagrams from a dozen originally separate manuscripts by different authors.

A change in the definition of a published work would obviously have a profound impact on a research library's role in supporting instruction and research. It is very clear that the "assembly" of information to support research will be simplified by the avail-- ability of discipline--oriented "electronic libraries" of current or retrospective information, searchable through formal indexing and natural language search keys of a scope and depth now out of reach, and retrievable immediately either as single units of infor-- mation or as user--designed products selected from the chapters, appendices, tables, structure diagrams, introductions, journal articles, technical reports, etc., of the original electronic manuscripts.

An understanding of the complexity of the process of moving research libraries into this scenario for the information age is of crucial importance to scholars and university administrators, as well as to librarians. The complexity of the process does not rest with the technology. The difficulty lies in part with the nature of the infrastructure of the highly--decentralized publishing industry, together with the need to resolve legal issues, such as copyright ownership and payment of authors and other stakeholders.

Another major set of issues deals with the philosophical -- as well as economic -- points of view which will crucially impact the design, pricing, and marketing of new information products. No one is so naive as to assume that publishers share with potential consumers in the research library marketplace a set of common values and interests. It should not be assumed that investors, mana-- gers, product designers, and marketing specialists will quickly offer information products which academic "consumers" – that is, stu-- dents, faculty, and research staff -- will find attractive when com--

pared with conventional books and journals. It is unknown whether the costs of initial investment by publishers in product design and equipment, of mass storage, of telecommunications, and costs to libraries for equipment and personnel for on–site search and retrieval, will allow publishers to offer electronic information pro–ducts for the academic market at a price which will allow them to gain a significant market share in competition with conventional books and journals. It is, moreover, unknown whether publishers will want to market them in competition with conventional pro–ducts. It may be more profitable, from the publisher's point of view, to price electronic information products so that they do not diminish the market for conventional books and journals.

Neither should it be assumed without question that the consumer will accept the electronic information systems and products des–cribed here. Microform publication was once proclaimed as a solu–tion to the problems of the cost of, and access to, the information resources needed by research libraries. Academic consumers, how–ever, have rejected microform except as a marginal supplement to conventional publishing. The minimum requirements for success–ful penetration of the academic market in competition with books and journals are the acceptance by publishers of industry–wide standards, and product design and pricing for a mass academic market.

It is useful to recognize the long term evolutionary nature of the changes described here. A generation of change is the realistic time scale. The horizons of strategic planning for research libraries must be pushed further into the future than is normally the case, even beyond the 15–20 year range. If a creative mix of conventional and non–traditional information sources is to be expected for 15–20 years, there will be a continued need for investment in both modes of information delivery for the foreseeable future.

Consider the following best case schedule for the development of a major market share for electronic publishing, based on the keystone of a standard for the preparation of electronic manuscripts.

Best Case Schedule for Development of Major
Academic Market Share for Electronic Publishing

Stage 1 1983   Contract awarded to consultant to draft
                       information industry standard for electronic
                       manuscript preparation.

                       Electronic publishing already occupies a
                       small but expanding market segment, e.g.,
                       law, chemistry.

90

Stage 2 1984–85   Electronic manuscript standards project com-- pleted through stage of stakeholders "en- dorsement" of draft ANSI standard.

Electronic publishing products continue to be produced to test the market.

Stage 3 1986–88   Formal approval process for ANSI standard completed.

Stakeholders negotiate economic issues.

Libraries expand access to non–standard electronic publishing.

Stage 4 1988–90   Publishers phase out or adapt existing photo-- composition equipment and software.

Non--standard electronic publishing programs are adapted to the standard.

New equipment and software is designed, manufactured, and acquired by publishers.

Electronic information products are designed.

Pricing and marketing strategies are devel-- oped.

Potential markets are determined.

Decisions are made on amounts of investment capital and on cost recovery time periods.

Stage 5 1988--   Consumer decisions impact marketplace.

Market shares of information products in electronic and hard copy are decided by consumers in the research library market.

Some electronic information products are selected as sole source, others are selected as a supplement to hard copy.

Stage 6 1990–2015   Electronic publishing products hypothetically

capture between 15% and 50% of the academic research library market.

Based on the median acquisition rate of
65,000 volumes per year in ARL libraries
in 1983, the median ARL library will divide
its acquisitions as follows.

Electronic Market Share	Hard Copy Volumes	Electronic Products Equivalent
15% share	55,250 volumes per year	9,750 volumes
25% share	48,750 volumes per year	16,250 volumes
50% share	32,500 volumes per year	32,500 volumes

This projection is, to understate the situation, very hypothetical.
Some might call it visionary. To inject a strong dose of reality,
let us consider the twenty–year history of the computerization
of the bibliographic apparatus of research libraries. This is a success
story, and is the result of technological and organizational innova-
tion – with a strong backbone of entrepreneurship – by librarians
working within a shared set of values from the 1960's to the 1980's.
One of the principal values underlying this innovative use of technology was to improve the cost efficiency of libraries.

As a result of this effort, all of the major research libraries
and hundreds of smaller academic libraries are linked into national
on–line computerized networks, connected by the public–switched
telephone network. These electronic networks carry tens of millions
of transactions annually, affecting positively the speed, efficiency,
and cost of acquiring and processing books and journals, identifying
and requesting books for interlibrary loan, and handling other
operations underlying the services of research libraries.

All of this cooperative activity is based on the creation in the
1960's of ANSI standards for encoding bibliographic data for all
types of library applications. These standard communications
formats are now used internationally by libraries in almost every
nation in North America and Western Europe. National computing
agencies such as OCLC and RLG/RLIN, organized by librarians
and supported on a non–profit basis, have developed bibliographic
data files in the world. (The largest files are those of the combined
computerized reservations systems of all U.S. airlines.)

These standard communications formats have also made possible
the development at reasonable cost of sophisticated computerized
library systems for research libraries. Such systems can thus be
linked directly through standard telecommunications protocols

to OCLC and RLIN. Through the public–switched network, each research library is also linked electronically to terminals in thousands of other U.S. libraries, using the same standard protocols, for resource sharing through interlibrary loan agreements.

All of this progress has been the work of library and information science professionals, working cooperatively within professional associations, in non–profit agencies, and with the Library of Congress and the National Library of Medicine. These pioneering efforts in the technology of information transfer have been based, to repeat, on the development of standards and their use by librarians and others within a set of widely shared professional goals and values, in a non–profit environment.

At this stage, research libraries have as a result carried the *research and development* phase of the computerization of library bibliographic records and related services, both nationally and locally, as far as is needed at this time. The *applications* phase for this R & D will extend for most libraries at least through 1990.

Research libraries will be profoundly changed as these applications are put in place in the 1985–90 period. But the still more important tasks of creating electronic data bases of full–text information, and the secondary work of organizing campus–level local area networks in which this data can be used, still are ahead. In this next phase of research library development, then, the challenge is (1) to apply to the full text of books, journals, and other library resources the process of developing standards for encoding and formatting data in electronic form, (2) to use the standards to develop systems for transmitting the full text from point to point, and (3) to develop methods of linking the sophisticated bibliographic systems of research libraries, and of abstracting and indexing agencies, to the full–text data. When this complex process is complete, it will be possible to put in place the library component of the hypothetical "integrated academic information center."

Investment capital decisions made by foundations and through Federal programs of assistance to libraries will be of profound importance to the effective application of electronic publishing to research libraries. These investment decisions will shape the future effectiveness of research libraries on every campus. It is time to question the wisdom of using such limited investment funds to shore up research library models which are limited in their effectiveness by basic structural characteristics. A fully computerized research library in 1984 terms, operating at optimum efficiency, represents a remarkable advance over its predecessors. Yet even this model should be regarded as a temporary stage, with a desirable maximum life span of 10–15 years. When capital investments are made at the national level or profession–wide level, the

decision-points should include the option of maintenance-level fund--
ing from local sources for conventional research library models,
and major investment in the development of advanced academic
information centers, in which full–text electronic publishing pro--
ducts are a key component.

The challenge to research libraries and to the community of
scholars and researchers is to forge links with this new electronic
information technology. It is in everyone's interest that the opportunities it presents should not weaken the research library either
in the near or long–term as an essential intermediary in the chain
of producing and disseminating information. Nor should the potential of this technological revolution be allowed to be reduced to
the status of the forgotten revolution of microform publishing.
All of the players in the campus community -- scholars, students,
and librarians -- have a direct interest in the result.

Furthermore, the decisions made in corporate and government
offices on the the design, marketing, and pricing of electronic infor--
mation products are of such importance that a case can be made
for seeking a consensus information policy in which all parties
will have a voice and will reap a share of the rewards. Even if such
planning for information policy is limited to the professional associations of the major scholarly and research disciplines, the long--
term rewards should be very significant.

In January 1984, after leaving a meeting on standards for elec--
tronic publishing, my wife and I drove to Capitol Hill to a reception
in the Great Hall of the Library of Congress. Two books are on
permanent exhibition in this grand hall of marble, of carved columns,
and a painted dome. On the right just before entering the Main
Reading Room is the Giant Bible of Mainz. It is a gloriously beautiful manuscript which a 15th century scribe took 14 months to --
almost -- complete. On the left side of the Hall if one of three
perfect copies of vellum of the Gutenberg Bible, the most famous
product of the age of the invention of printing. It was difficult
to put away the thought that another revolution in disseminating
the written record was possible, and was waiting for the moment
when the technological means and creative minds came together.

Issues in Access to Scholarly Information

A Bibliography

Robert A. Seal

Introduction

The primary mission of academic research libraries is to provide information to faculty, students, and staff in support of research, teaching, and study. To succeed in this goal, librarians must be concerned with ensuring and enhancing both physical and bibliographic access to local and national resources. Within our own collections, books, journals, and numerous nonbook materials must be easy to identify, locate, and obtain for use. Resources not held locally must be readily identifiable and rapidly procured as cost-effectively as possible. Difficulties and delays in accessing scholarly information held in research collections must be minimized, not only to satisfy the needs of individuals, whether for research, classroom preparation, or administrative decisionmaking, but also to guarantee that the educational goals of the institution itself are realized. Rogers and Weber, in their classic *University Library Administration* (1971), wrote that

"The most significant step the library can take in fostering general education is to provide freedom of access to collections. The ease with which one can reach the collections will affect one's attitudes. This is true of research collections as well as those specifically for undergraduate needs."

Though providing access to scholarly information has always provided academic librarians with challenges, it has been become even more difficult in the past decade. Shrinking or nearly static budgets have adversely affected staffing levels, acquisitions, and operations which in turn affect the ability to provide effective access to information. The topic in question is broad and complex with a number of important issues and aspects. The papers in this volume address a number of the issues related to providing access to scholarly information, as well as problems which stand in the way of effectively achieving this goal. Physical arrangement of collections and buildings, collection development, reference service, preservation, technical services, online catalogs, networks, copyright and fair use, and recent technological developments are just a few of the topics related to access to scholarly information.

The bibliography below provides a list of citations for the reader interested in exploring these issues in more depth. It is selective rather than comprehensive, meant to provide citations to key papers, books, and reports in the field. Since librarianship in general is concerned with acquiring and disseminating information, many of its aspects conceivably have relevance to access to scholarly information. However, since scholarly information implies issues related to academic and research libraries, the references have been limited for the most part to those issues related to college and university libraries.

The bibliography generally is limited to the last ten years of the literature and is divided into seven parts: I. General; II. Build-ings, physical facilities, and collection arrangement; III. Services, collections, and preservation; IV. Technical services; V. Networks and cooperative efforts; VI. Copyright and related issues; VII. Tech-nological developments. Each section has a short introduction describing the contents of the books, articles, and reports listed.

General

Included here are articles, reports, and books of a general nature on the topic of access to scholarly information, as well as references which cover more than one aspect of the topic and which could not easily be assigned to one of the other sections below. Several references on scholarly communication are given, too, for the two subjects are closely allied in terms of access to and the transmission of ideas and facts. Included here, and in other sections, are refer-ences from the journal *Scholarly Publishing* which contains a great deal of relevant information on the dissemination of scholarly knowledge, whether by libraries or publishers.

Published policy guidelines regarding access to different types of academic library collections, for example those issued by the American Library Association and its subdivisions or the Society of American Archivists, are included as illustrations of efforts made to formalize and insure access to information. Other issues affecting access, such as community use of academic libraries, subject access, and privacy issues are also presented.

Abell, Millicent D., and Coolman, Jacqueline M. "Professionalism and Productivity: Keys to the Future of Academic Library and Information Services." *New Directions in Higher Education* no. 39 (Priorities for Academic Libraries). 10 (1982):71--86.

American Library Association. Association of College and Research Libraries. Committee on Community Use of Academic Libraries. "Draft: Access Policy Guidelines." *College & Research Libraries News,* no. 5 (1975), 167--69.

American Library Association. Association of College and Research Libraries. Rare Books and Manuscripts Section. Manuscripts Collections Committee and Society of American Archivists. Committee on Reference and Access Policies. "Joint Statement on Access to Original Research Materials." *College & Research Libraries News,* no. 4 (1979):111--12.

American Library Association. Council. "Administrative Policies and Procedures Affecting Access to Library Resources and Services: An Interpretation of the Library Bill of Rights; adopted January 27, 1982." *Newsletter on Intellectual Freedom* 31 (1982):36+.

American Library Association. Council. "Restricted Access to Library Materials; Library Bill of Rights Revised Interpretation, amended July 1, 1981." *American Libraries* 12 (1981):495--96.

Arms, William Y. "Scholarly Information." *EDUCOM* 18, no. 3--4 (1984):21--23.

Association of Research Libraries. Office of Management Studies. *Corporate Use of Research Libraries.* ARL SPEC Kit no. 88. October 1982.

Beckman, Margaret. "Problems of Library Facilities in Research Environments." *Journal of the Society of Research Administrators* 12 (1980):11--15.

Berry, John. "Access: The Top Priority." *Library Journal* 106 (1981):397. Discussion: 106 (1981):1147, 1255, 1351, 1857.

Bloss, Meredith. "Research; and Standards for Library Service." *Library Research* 2 (1980):285--308.

Borkowski, Casimir, and Macleod, Murdo J. "The Implications of Some Recent Studies of Library Use." *Scholarly Publishing* 11 (1979):3--24.

Boylan, Ray. "Scholarly Citadel in Chicago: The Centries." *Wilson Library Bulletin* 53 (1979):503--06.

Budington, William S. "The Independent Research Library. Related paper no. 4." Washington, DC: National Commission on Libraries and Information Science, National Program for Library and Information Services, 1974. ED 100 390.

Burke, John Gordon, and Bowers, H. Paxton. "Institutional Censorship." *Library Journal* 95 (1970):468–69.

Cochrane, Pauline. "Improving the Quality of Information Retrieval--Online to a Library Catalog or Other Access Service . . . Or . . . Where Do We Go from Here?" *Online* 5 (1981):30–42.

Cole, John Y. "Books, Libraries, and Scholarly Traditions." *Scholarly Publishing* 13 (1981):31–43.

Cuadra, Carlos A. et al. "A Library and Information Science Research Agenda for the 1980s: Summary Report." *Library Research* 4 (1982):235--77.

Daval, Nicola, ed. "Prospects for Improving Document Delivery. Minutes of the Semiannual Meeting (101st, Arlington, VA, October 13–14, 1982)." Washington, DC; Association of Research Libraries, 1983. ED 234 785.

de Gennaro, Richard. "Libraries and Networks in Transition: Problems and Prospects for the 1980's." *Library Journal* 106 (1981):1045--49.

Dix, W.S. "Access to Manuscripts Collections." *AB Bookman's Weekly* 54(1974):755+.

Foskett, A.C. *The Subject Approach to Information.* 4th ed. London: Clive Bingley; Hamden, CT: Linnet Books, 1982.

Frick, E., ed. "Access to Information." *Cornell University Library Bulletin* April 1972 issue.

Frugé, August. "Beyond Publishing: A System of Scholarly Writing and Reading." *Scholarly Publishing* 9 (1978):291–311.

Fry, Bernard M. "Public Access Via Depository Libraries: Federal, State, and Local." *Drexel Library Quarterly* 16 (1980):104–17.

Haas, Warren. "Research Libraries and the Dynamics of Change."
Scholarly Publishing 11 (1980):195–202.

Hernon, Peter. *Public Access to Government Information; Issue,
Trends, and Strategies.* Norwood, NJ: Ablex Publishing Corp.,
1984.

Hyman, Richard J. "Access to Library Collections: Summary of
a Documentary and Opinion Survey on the Direct Shelf Approach and Browsing." *Library Resources & Technical Services*
15 (1971):479–91.

Jordan, R.T. *Tomorrow's Library; Direct Access and Delivery.*
New York: R.R. Bowker, 1970.

Kaser, D.E. "Library Access and the Mobility of Users." *College
& Research Libraries* 35 (1974):280–84.

Kerr, Chester. "A National Enquiry into the Production and Dissemination of Scholarly Knowledge." *Scholarly Publishing*
7 (1975):3–13.

Lawrence, M. Therese. "Are Resource Treasures Hidden From
Scholars in Our Libraries? What is the Access to Ephemera?"
Special Libraries 64 (1973):285–90.

Levin, Marc A. "Access and Dissemination Issues Concerning Federal Government Information." *Special Libraries* 74 (1983):127–
37.

Machlup, Fritz. *Information Through the Printed Word; The Dissemination of Scholarly, Scientific, and Intellectual Knowledge.*
4v. New York: Praeger, 1978–80.

Manten, Arie A. "Possible Future Relevance of Publishing Primary
Scholarly Information in the Form of Synopses." *Journal
of Information Science* 1 (1980):293–96.

Miller, Nancy. "Public Access to Public Records: Some Threatening
Reforms." *Wilson Library Bulletin* 56 (1981):95–99.

Milstead, Jessica L. *Subject Access Systems; Alternatives in Design.*
New York: Academic Press, 1984.

Najarian, Suzanne E. "Organizational Factors in Human Memory:

Implications for Library Organization and Access Systems." *Library Quarterly* 51 (1981):269–91.

"National Perspectives for ARL Libraries. Minutes of the Semi-Annual Meeting of the Association of Research Libraries (86th, Houston, Texas, May 8–9, 1975)." Washington, DC: Association of Research Libraries, 1975. ED 129 261.

Nolan, Marianne. "Library Access for Students in Nontraditional Degree Programs." *Drexel Library Quarterly* 11 (1975):16–33.

Praeger, Frederick A. "Librarians, Publishers, and Scholars, Common Interests, Different Views: The View of an Independent Scholarly Publisher." *Library Quarterly* 54 (1984):21–29.

"Publishers and Libraries; A Foundation for Dialogue." Proceedings of the Forty-second Conference of the Graduate School, May 13–15, 1983. *Library Quarterly* 54, no. 1, January 1984 issue.

"Question of Access." In *History of the Principles of Librarianship*, by James Thompson, pp. 62–85. London: Clive Bingley, 1977.

Ratcliffe, F.W. "Problems of Open Access in Large Academic Libraries." *Libri* 18 (1968):95–111.

Scholarly Communication; The Report of the National Enquiry. Baltimore, MD: The Johns Hopkins University Press, 1979.

"Scholars' Access to Information: Public Responsibility/Private Initiative. Minutes of the Ninety-ninth Meeting, October 29–30, 1981, Washington, DC." Washington, DC: Association of Research Libraries, 1982. ED 215 691.

"Scholar's Right to Know Versus the Individual's Right to Privacy." Proceedings of the First Rockefeller Archive Center Conference, December 5, 1975. New York: Rockefeller University Press, 1976.

"Security Problems Prod Princeton to Impose Access Curbs." *Library Journal* 106 (1981):2171.

Society of American Archivists. "Standards for Access to Research Materials in Archival and Manuscript Repositories." *American Archivist* 37 (1974):153–54.

Soper, Mary Ellen. "Characteristics and Use of Personal Collections." *Library Quarterly* 46 (1976):397--415.

Stambrook, F.G. "Changing Climate of Opinion about University
Libraries." *Canadian Library Journal* 40 (1983):273--76.

Taylor, Alan R. "The Changing Fortunes of Academic Libraries."
Scholarly Publishing 10 (1978):45--53.

Weinberg, Charles B. "The University Library: Analysis and Proposals. Research Paper Number 169." Stanford, CA: Stanford
University, Graduate School of Business, 1973. ED 087 405.

Wiseman, John A. "Community Use of University Libraries."
Canadian Library Journal 32 (1975):373--76.

Buildings, Physical Facilities, and Collection Arrangement

Physical access to materials is the theme of this portion of
the bibliography. Citations here focus on the planning, design,
and arrangement of library buildings and collections to ease and
expedite access to information in academic libraries. Also of interest
are problems encountered by users in attempting to locate and use
resources including those faced by physically disabled students
and faculty. Other selected issues described by the references
in this section are book availability, the effect of open stacks on
access, and integrating automation into the planning of an academic
library to facilitate use and ensure access.

Association of Research Libraries. Office of Management Studies.
Physical Access. ARL SPEC Kit no. 27. June 1976, updated
1978.

Association of Research Libraries. Office of Management Studies.
Services to the Disabled in ARL Libraries. ARL SPEC Kit no.
81. February 1982.

Atkinson, Hugh C. "Optimum Speed of Library Access as Related
to Optimum Size of Library Collections. Final Report."
Columbus, OH: Ohio State University Libraries, 1970. ED
148 345.

Beckman, Margaret. "Library Buildings in the Network Environ--
ment." *Journal of Academic Librarianship* 9 (1983):281--84.

Begg, R.T. "Disabled Libraries: An Examination of Physical and Attitudinal Barriers to Handicapped Library Users." *Law Library Journal* 72 (1980):513--25.

Buckland, Michael H. *Book Availability and the Library User.* New York: Pergamon, 1975.

Cohen, Aaron, and Cohen, Elaine. *Designing and Space Planning for Libraries; A Behavioral Guide.* New York: Bowker, 1979.

Cohen, Elaine, and Cohen, Aaron. *Automation, Space Management, and Productivity.* New York: Bowker, 1982.

Collins, A. "Planning the Library for Use." In *Medical Librarianship,* pp. 153--70. London: Library Association, 1981.

Conn, D.R., and McCallum, B. "Design for Accessibility." *Canadian Library Journal* 39 (1982):119--25.

Freeman, Michael. "College Library Buildings in Transition: A Study of 36 Libraries Built in 1967--68." *College & Research Libraries* 43 (1982):478--80.

Frohmberg, K.A. et al. "Increases in Book Availability in a Large College Library." In American Society for Information Science. Conference, Anaheim, Calif., 1980. Proceedings, v. 17: *Communicating Information,* pp. 292--94. White Plains, NY: Knowledge Industry Publications for ASIS, 1980.

International Federation of Library Associations. "Library Buildings Section. Papers." Papers presented at the 48th Annual Meeting of the International Federation of Library Associations (Montreal, Canada, August 22--28, 1982). August 1982. ED 227 876.

Lock, R.N. "Arrangement of Books for Use." In *Manual of Library Economy,* pp. 208--22. Hamden, CT: Shoestring; London: Clive Bingley; 1977.

Metcalf, Keyes D. *Planning Academic and Research Libraries.* New York: McGraw--Hill, 1965.

Myers, J. "Designing Open--Stack Areas for the User." In *Sign Systems for Libraries: Solving the Wayfinding Problem,* pp. 195--201. New York: R.R. Bowker, 1979.

Orne, Jerrold. "Library Building Trends and Their Meanings."
Library Journal 102 (1977):2397--401.

Reynolds, Catherine J. "Planning Space for the Government Docu--
ments Collection in Research Libraries." Washington, DC:
Council on Library Resources, 1977. ED 152 310.

Rovelstad, Mathilde V. "Open Shelves/Closed Shelves in Research
Libraries." *College & Research Libraries* 37 (1976):457--67.

"Sharing Building Space; Decentralization for Access." *Library
Journal* 105 (1980):143--44.

Shill, Harold B. "Open Stacks and Library Performance." *College
& Research Libraries* 41 (1980):220--26. Discussion: 41 (1980):
527--28; 42 (1981):250--52.

Snyder, Richard L. "College Library Buildings in Transition --
Looking at the 1980's." Talk delivered before the Conference
on College and Academic Library Buildings in the 80's (New
Stanton, Penn., October 14--15, 1983). ED 241 057.

Vasi, John. "Building Libraries for the Handicapped; A Second
Look." *Journal of Academic Librarianship* 2 (1976):82--83.

Velleman, Ruth A. "Architectural and Program Accessibility:
A Review of Library Programs, Facilities and Publications
for Librarians Serving Disabled Individuals." *Drexel Library
Quarterly* 16 (1980):32--47.

Wilson, Betty Ruth. "Library Accessibility." Paper presented
at the Conference on Academic Library Services to Disabled
Students (Tallahassee, Florida, May 6--7, 1983). May 1983.
ED 240 759.

Services, Collections, and Preservation

How scholarly information is acquired, serviced, and preserved
is the theme of this section. References deal with the impact of
collection development, reference service, and conservation activity
on access to library resources. Bibliographic, rather than physical,
access is of critical concern here, with emphasis on how libraries
and librarians best solve this dilemma. Subject access, through
traditional and automated catalogs, is also a key issue, as is the
integration of online and traditional reference services. Developing

collections as a component of providing access to scholarly informa-tion is a theme frequently addressed in the literature, as is preserva--tion, in particular the conflict between the need to protect resources, especially rare books and manuscripts, and the need to provide physical access for scholars.

Aguolu, C.C. "Aspects of the Problems of Bibliographic Access to University Library Collections." *International Library Review* 11 (1979):225--43.

Association of Research Libraries. Office of Management Studies. *Basic Preservation Procedures.* ARL SPEC Kit no. 70. January 1981.

Association of Research Libraries. Office of Management Studies. *Planning for Preservation.* ARL SPEC Kit no. 66. July--August 1980.

Association of Research Libraries. Office of Management Studies. *Special Collections.* ARL SPEC Kit no. 57. September 1979.

Baker, B., and Kluegel, K. "Availability and Use of OCLC for Reference in Large Academic Libraries." *RQ* 21 (1982):379–83.

Blood, Richard W. "Impact of OCLC on Reference Service." *Jour--nal of Academic Librarianship* 3 (1977):68--73.

Chaloner, Kathryn, and De Klerk, Ann. "A Comparison of Two Current Awareness Methods." Paper presented at the Annual Meeting of the American Library Association (New York, NY, June 1980). June 1980. ED 201 329.

Culkin, Patricia B. "Computer--Based Public Access Systems: A Forum for Library Instruction." *Drexel Library Quarterly* 16 (1980):69--82.

de Gennaro, Richard. "Impact of On--line Services on the Academic Library." In *On--line Revolution in Libraries: Proceedings of the 1977 conference in Pittsburgh, Pa.,* edited by Allen Kent and Thomas J. Galvin, pp. 177--81. New York: Marcel Dekker, 1978.

De Somogyi, A. "Access Versus Preservation." *Canadian Library Journal* 31 (1974):414--15+.

Dougherty, Richard M. "Preservation and Access: A Collision of Objectives." *Journal of Academic Librarianship* 8 (1982): 199.

Droessler, J.B., and Rholes, J.M. "Online Services at the Reference Desk: DIALOG, RLIN and OCLC." *Online* 7 (1983):79–86.

Frankie, Suzzane O. "Collection Development in Academic Libraries." *Catholic Library World* 54 (1982):103–09.

Greene, R. *Faculty Acceptance and Use of a System Providing Remote Bibliographic and Physical Access to an Academic Book Collection.* Ph.D. dissertation. Florida State University, 1973.

Haas, Warren J. "Preparation of Detailed Specifications for a National System for the Preservation of Library Materials. Final Report." Washington, DC: Association of Research Libraries, 1972. ED 060 908.

Hamman, E.G. "Access to Information: A Reconsideration of the Service Goals of a Small Urban College Library." In American Library Association. Association of College and Research Libraries. *New Horizons for Academic Libraries,* edited by Robert D. Johnson Stueart and Richard David, pp. 534–38. New York: K.G. Sauer, 1979.

Hoadley, Irene Braden. "The Undergraduate Library – The First 20 Years." Paper prepared for the Institute on Training for Service in Undergraduate Libraries, August 17–21, 1970. San Diego, CA: University of California, San Diego, Library, 1970. ED 042 478.

Hock, R.E. "Providing Access to Externally Available Bibliographic Data Bases in an Academic Library." *College & Research Libraries* 36 (1975):208–15.

Jackson, Angela R. Haygarth. "Online Information Handling – The User Perspective." *Online Review* 7 (1983):25–32.

Jones, D.H. "RLIN and OCLC as Reference Tools." *Journal of Library Automation* 14 (1981):201–02.

Klugman, S. "Online Information Retrieval Interface with Traditional Reference Services." Paper presented at the 3rd International Online Information Meeting, London, December 1979. *Online Review* 4 (1980):263–72.

Line, M.B. "Access to Collections, Including Interlibrary Loan." In *Aspects of Library Development Planning,* pp. 74–92. Bronx, NY: Mansell, 1983.

Lucker, Jay K. "Library Resources and Bibliographic Control." *College & Research Libraries* 40 (1979):141–53.

McDonald, R.R. et al. "Research Libraries Information Network as a Public Service Tool at Stanford University Libraries." *Reference Services Review* 9 (1981):33–37.

Magnuson, Barbara. "Collection Management: New Technology, New Decisions." *Wilson Library Bulletin* 57 (1983):736–41.

Mischo, W.H. "Expanded Subject Access to Library Collections Using Computer–Assisted Indexing Techniques." In American Society for Information Science. Conference, Anaheim, Calif., 1980. Proceedings, v. 17: *Communicating Information,* pp. 155–57. White Plains, NY: Knowledge Industry Publications for ASIS, 1980.

Munn, Robert F. "Collection Development vs. Resource Sharing: The Dilemma of the Middle–Level Institutions." *Journal of Academic Librarianship* 8 (1983):352–53.

Osburn, Charles B. *Academic Research and Library Resources: Changing Patterns in America.* Westport, CT: Greenwood Press, 1979.

Smith, John Brewster, and Schleifer, Harold B. "Research Libraries in Transition: What Faculty Members Should Know About Changing Patterns of Library Service." *AAUP Bulletin* 64 (1978):78–81.

Stevens, N.D. "Role of Networks in the Preservation of Library Materials." *Journal of Academic Librarianship* 7 (1981):171–72.

Studdiford, Abigail. "Historical Review of Projects Funded Under Title II–C of the Higher Education Act of 1965: Strengthening Research Library Resources, 1978–1981." Washington, DC: Office of Libraries and Learning Technologies (ED), 1982. ED 227 863.

Walker, Gay. "Preservation Efforts in Larger U.S. Academic Libraries." *College & Research Libraries* 36 (1975):39–44.

Wilson, A. "For This and Future Generations: Managing the Conflict Between Conservation and Use." *Library Review* 31 (1982):163–72.

Technical Services

There have been two significant developments in technical services in the last decade which have substantially affected libraries' ability to deal with access to scholarly information: the revised edition of the *Anglo–American Cataloging Rules* (AACR2) and the advent of the online catalog. Those two events have overshadowed any other technical services factors which may have affected access, and this is quickly evident from the bibliography which follows. And while AACR2 has had a noticeable effect on access because of closed or frozen catalogs and changes in headings, the major impact has been the online catalog. It has, and will, revolutionize access to local collections through multiple access points, fast turnaround, ease of use, and decentralized access. The references here discuss planning, implementation, and use of the online catalog, as well as user reaction, problems, and future prospects. Another topic covered is access to the periodical literature, a dilemma different from those related to identifying monographic works.

Association of Research Libraries. Office of Management Studies. *Online Catalogs.* ARL SPEC Kit no. 96. July–August 1983.

Association of Research Libraries. Office of Management Studies. *Planning for the Future of the Card Catalog.* ARL SPEC Kit no. 46. July 1978.

Atkinson, Hugh C. "Electronic Catalog." In *Nature and Future of the Catalog,* ed. by Maurice J. Freedman and S. Michael Malinconico, pp. 102–13. Phoenix, AZ: Oryx Press, 1979.

Beckman, Margaret M. "Online Catalogs and Library Users." *Library Journal* 107 (1982):2043–47.

Benedict Betty Z. "Changing Patterns of Access to Periodical Literature." *Serials Librarian* 6, no. 2–3 (Winter 1981/Spring 1982):27–38.

Bishop, D.F. "CLR Online Public Access Catalog Study: Analysis of ARL User Responses." *Information Technology and Libraries* 2 (1983):315–21.

Broadus, R.N. "Online Catalogs and Their Users." *College & Research Libraries* 44 (1983):458–67.

Brownrigg, Edwin B., and Lynch, Clifford A. "Online Catalogs: Through a Glass Darkly." *Information Technology and Libraries* 2 (1983):104–15.

Bullock, Connie et al. "State of the Art and Alternatives. Subgroup B; Interim Report." Prepared by the UCLA (Library) Working Group on Public Catalogs. July 1974. ED 121 324.

Chervinko, J.S. "Online COM Catalog to Revolutionize Library Service." *Journal of Micrographics* 15 (1982):30–32.

Cochrane, Pauline A.A. "Modern Subject Access in the Online Age." *American Libraries* 15 (1984):80–83; 145–48+; 250–52; 336–39.

Cochrane, Pauline A. "Subject Access in the Online Catalog." Dublin, OH: OCLC, Inc., 1982. ED 215 686.

Cochrane, Pauline A. Atherton, and Markey, Karen. "Catalog Use Studies -- Since the Introduction of Online Interactive Catalogs: Impact on Design for Subject Access." *Library and Information Science Research* 5 (1983):337–63.

Corbin, John, ed. "Proceedings of the Preconference on Online Catalogs (Houston, Texas, March 31, 1981)." Texas Library Association. March 1982. ED 217 842.

Dougherty, Richard M., and Blomquist, Laura L. *Improving Access to Library Resources: The Influence of Organization of Library Collections, and of User Attitudes Toward Innovative Services.* Metuchen, NJ: The Scarecrow Press, 1974.

Dwyer, James R. "The Effect of Closed Catalogs on Public Access." Paper presented at the Annual Conference of the American Library Association (Dallas, Texas, June 24, 1979). ED 190 142.

Dwyer, James R. "The Effect of Closed Catalogs on Public Access." *Library Resources & Technical Services* 25 (1981):186–95.

Fayen, Emily G. *Online Catalog: Improving Public Access to Library Materials.* White Plains, NY: Knowledge Industry Publications, 1983.

Ferguson, Douglas. "Online Catalogs at the Reference Desk and Beyond." *RQ* 20 (Fall 1980):7–10.

Ferguson, Douglas et al. "CLR Public Online Catalog Study: An Overview." *Information Technology and Libraries* 1 (1982): 84–97.

Ferguson, Douglas et al. "Public Online Catalogs and Research Libraries. Final Report." Stanford, CA: Research Libraries Group, 1982. ED 229 014.

Freedman, Maurice J., and Malinconico, S. Michael, eds. *Nature and Future of the Catalog; Proceedings of the ALA's Information Science and Automation Division's 1975 and 1977 Institutes on the Catalog.* Phoenix, AZ: Oryx Press, 1979.

Freiburger, Gary A. "The Online Catalog: More Than a Catalog Online." *Catholic Library World* 55 (1983):213–15.

Golden, G.A. et al. "Patron Approaches to Serials: A User Study." *College & Research Libraries* 43 (1982):22–30.

Hildreth, Charles R. *Online Public Access Catalogs: The User Interface.* Dublin, OH: OCLC, Office of Research, 1982.

Horny, Karen L. "Online Catalogs: Coping with the Choices." *Journal of Academic Librarianship* 8 (1982):14–19.

Kaske, N.K., and Sanders, N.P. "Evaluating the Effectiveness of Subject Access: The View of the Library Patron." In American Society for Information Science. Conference, Anaheim, Calif., 1980. Proceedings, v. 17: *Communicating Information,* pp. 323–25. White Plains, NY: Knowledge Industry Publications, 1980.

Kilgour, Fred G. "Design of Online Catalogs." In *Nature and Future of the Catalog,* edited by Maurice J. Freedman and S. Michael Malinconico, pp. 34–45. Phoenix, AZ: Oryx Press, 1979.

Krikelas, James. "Searching the Library Catalog – A Study of

Users' Access." *Library Research* 2 (1980):215–30.

Lipow, Anne Grodzins. "Practical Considerations of the Current Capabilities of Subject Access in Online Public Catalogs." *Library Resources & Technical Services* 27 (1983):81–87.

McClintock, Marsha Hamilton, ed. "Training Users of Online Public Access Catalogs. Report of a conference sponsored by Trinity University and the Council on Library Resources (San Antonio, Texas, January 12–14, 1983)." Washington, DC: Council on Library Resources, Inc., 1983. ED 235 832.

McClure, Charles R. "Subject and Added Entries As Access to Information." *Journal of Academic Librarianship* 2 (1976): 9–14.

Matthews, Joseph R. "Online Public Access Catalogs: Assessing the Potential." *Library Journal* 107 (1982): 1067–71.

Matthews, Joseph R. *A Study of Six Online Public Access Catalogs: A Review of Findings, Final Report.* Grass Valley, CA: Matthews (Joseph R.) and Associates, 1982. ED 231 389.

Moore, Carol Weiss. "User Reactions to Online Catalogs: An Exploratory Study." *College & Research Libraries* 42 (1981): 295–302.

Murfin, M.E. "Myth of Accessibility: Frustration and Failure in Retrieving Periodicals." *Journal of Academic Librarianship* 6 (1980):16–19.

"Preconference Institute on Prospects for the Online Catalog, Philadelphia, 1982. Papers." *Library Resources & Technical Services* 27 (1983):4–75.

Regan, Lee, and Olivetti, L. James. "Access to Periodical Indexes and Abstracts in Academic Libraries: A Survey." *Serials Librarian* 6, no. 2–3 (Winter 1981/Spring 1982):39–45.

Richards, Timothy F. "The Online Catalog: Issues in Planning and Development." *Journal of Academic Librarianship* 10 (1984):4–9.

Rowley, J.E. "Online Catalogue Prospects: A Review." *Library Review* 31 (1982):261–67.

Scilken, M.H. "Catalog As a Public Service Tool." In *Nature and Future of the Catalog,* edited by Maurice J. Freedman and S. Michael Malinconico, pp. 89--101. Phoenix, AZ: Oryx Press, 1979.

Seal, Alan. "Experiments With Full and Short Entry Catalogues: A Study of Library Needs." *Library Resources & Technical Services* 27 (1983):144--55.

Steinberg, D., and Metz, P. "User Response to and Knowledge About an Online Catalog." *College & Research Libraries* 45 (1984):66–70.

Wilson, P. "Catalog as Access Mechanism: Background and Con--cepts." *Library Resources & Technical Services* 27 (1983): 4--17.

Networks and Cooperative Efforts

Resource sharing, of interest to academic and research libraries for many years, is the focus of this portion of the bibliography. Obtaining materials not held locally is an important concern since budgets, space, and staffing restrictions do not permit collections of unlimited size. The references here discuss networks and how they facilitate access to information through interlibrary loan, online data bases, and other means. The Association of Research Libraries have devoted a number of meetings to resource sharing and networking; references to the minutes of those sessions are included. National networks such as OCLC and the Research Libraries Group, and national resources such as the Center for Re--search Libraries, are also frequently discussed in the literature.

Association of Research Libraries. Office of Management Studies. *Resource Sharing.* ARL SPEC Kit no. 42. March 1978.

Babcock, Julie. "Cooperation Between Types of Libraries, 1968--1971; An Annotated Bibliography." Philadelphia, PA: Drexel University, Graduate School of Library Science, 1971. ED 057 879.

Battin, Patricia M. "Research Libraries in the Network Environ--ment: The Case for Cooperation." *Journal of Academic Li--brarianship* 6 (1980):68–73.

Berry, John. "Interlibrary Loan and the Network." *Library Journal*

103 (1978):795.

Butler, Brett. "A Nationwide Location Data Base and Service. Network Planning Paper Number 1, 1978." Los Altos, CA: Butler Associates, 1978. ED 168 515.

Davison, W.E. "WLN/RLG/LC Linked Systems Project." *Information Technologies and Libraries* 2 (1983):34–46.

de Gennaro, Richard. "Austerity, Technology, and Resource Sharing: Research Libraries Face the Future." *Library Journal* 100 (1975):917–23.

Hendricks, Donald D. "A Report on Library Networks." Champaign, IL: University of Illinois, Graduate School of Library Science, 1973. (Occasional Papers, no. 108). ED 092 094.

Jacob, Mary Ellen. "A National Interlibrary Loan Network: The OCLC Approach." *Bulletin of the American Society for Information Science* 5 (1979):24–25.

Jacob, Mary Ellen et al. "Online Resource Sharing II. A Comparison of: OCLC, Incorporated, Research Libraries Information Network, and Washington Library Network." San Jose, CA: California Library Authority for Systems and Services, 1979. ED 183 220.

Kronick, David A. "Goodbye to Farewells: Resource Sharing and Cost Sharing." *Journal of Academic Librarianship* 8 (1982): 132–36.

"Library Networking: Current Problems and Future Prospects!" Special conference issue containing seven papers and a panel discussion. *Resource Sharing and Information Networks* 1 (1983):6–139.

Little (Arthur D.) Inc. *A Comparative Evaluation of Alternative Systems for the Provision of Effective Access to Periodical Literature: A Report to the National Commission on Libraries and Information Science.* Washington, DC: The Commission, 1979.

McCoy, Richard. "Library Networking: Current Problems and Future Prospects." *Resource Sharing and Information Networks* 1 (1983):59–72.

McDonald, John P. "National Planning and Academic Libraries." Paper presented at the General Council Meeting of the International Federation of Library Associations (40th, Washington, DC, November 17--23, 1974). Washington, DC: Association of Research Libraries, 1974. ED 104 444.

Malinconico, S. Michael. "National Bibliographic Network: A Patrician Pursuit." *Library Journal* 105 (1980):1791–92.

Morgan, Candy et al. "Resources at the Top: Answers and Referrals." *RQ* 21 (1981):28--42.

"A National Program for the Association of Research Libraries. Minutes of the Meeting (79th, January 22, 1972, Chicago, Illinois)." Washington, DC: Association of Research Libraries, 1972. ED 082 787.

"New Opportunities for Research Libraries. Minutes of the Meeting (80th, May 12–13, 1972, Atlanta, Georgia)." Washington, DC: Association of Research Libraries, 1972. ED 082 788.

Palmour, Vernon E. "Effective Access to the Periodical Literature: A National Program." Washington, DC: National Commission on Libraries and Information Science, 1976. ED 148 342.

Pings, Vern M. "Directions and Limitations of Automated Library Systems. Working Paper No. 14." Detroit, MI: Wayne State University Libraries, 1979. ED 174 199.

"Research Libraries and Cooperative Systems. Minutes of the Semi--Annual Meeting of the Association of Research Libraries (88th, Seattle, Washington, May 6–7, 1976)." Washington, DC: Association of Research Libraries, 1976. ED 129 263.

Simpson, Donald B. "National Library and Information Service Network: A View From the Bottom." *Journal of Library Automation* 10 (1977):335–42.

Simpson, Donald B. et al. "Center for Research Libraries: Meeting the Opportunity to Fulfill the Promise: A Symposium." *Journal of Academic Librarianship* 9 (1983):258–69.

Smalley, Donald A. et al. "Linking the Bibliographic Utilities: Benefits and Costs. Technical Reports." Columbus, OH: Battelle Memorial Institute, 1980. ED 195 276.

The impact of copyright and fair use on access to scholarly information is the topic of this portion of the bibliography, with issues such as photocopying, reserves, interlibrary lending, and offprints being addressed. Included, too, are reports of the National Commission on New Technological Uses of Copyrighted Works (CONTU) which in 1975--1976 considered copyright for books, non--book materials, and computer software. Ownership and copy--right of machine--readable data is an emerging issue which will have effects on research libraries; of special interest is the recent attempt of OCLC to copyright its data base. This has a number of implications for academic libraries who need to insure access to scholarly information both locally and nationally. Copyright policies as they affect interlibrary loan are of concern, too, for they affect access to scholarly materials in a variety of ways.

American Library Association. Association of College and Research Libraries. Copyright Committee (ad hoc). "Copyright Con--troversy: Statement of the ACRL Committee on Copyright." *College & Research Libraries News* no. 8 (1981):288.

Association of Research Libraries. Office of Management Studies. *Copyright Policies.* ARL SPEC Kit. no. 102. March 1984.

Association of Research Libraries. Office of Management Studies. *Interlibrary Loan.* ARL SPEC Kit no. 92. March 1983.

Bush, G.P., and Dreyfuss, R.H., eds. *Technology and Copyright: Sources and Materials.* rev. ed. Mt. Airy, MD: Lomond Publi--cations, 1979.

Butler, M.A. "Copyright and Academic Library Photocopying." *College & Research Libraries News* no. 4 (1982):123--25.

Coleman, E. "Impact of Copyright on the Future of Scholarly Publishing." *Aslib Proceedings* 29 (1977):259--65. Also in *Library Literature 8 – The Best of 1977,* edited by William A. Katz, pp. 238--47. Metuchen, NJ: Scarecrow, 1978.

de Gennaro, Richard. "Copyright, Resource Sharing, and Hard Times: A View From the Field." *American Libraries* 8 (1977): 430--35.

Duchesne, R.M. et al. "Ownership of Machine--Readable Bibliogra--

phic Data. Canadian Network Papers Number 5." Ottawa: National Library of Canada, 1983. ED 231 396.

"Final Report of the National Commission on New Technological Uses of Copyrighted Works, Washington, DC." Washington, DC: National Commission on New Technological Uses of Copy-- righted Works, 1978. ED 160 122.

Flint, Carl, and Peters, Marybeth. "The Six Basic Needs of Educa-- tion Vs. Public Law 94–533 Copyright Act of 1976." Atlanta, GA; Public Health Service (DHEW), 1978. ED 188 617.

"Good Morning. © OCLC." *American Libraries* 14 (1983):74.

Holroyd, Michael. "Wrongs of Copyright." *Library Journal* 101 (1976):1081--83.

Hood, H.A. "Survey and Critique of Photocopying Provisions of the New American Copyright Act." *International Journal of Law Libraries* 6 (1979):159–69.

Hutchings, M. "Model Policy Concerning College and University Photocopying for Classroom, Research, and Library Reserve Use." *College & Research Libraries News* no. 4 (1982):127--31.

Little, Craig B., and Halley, Fred S. "Photocopying and the New Copyright Law." *Teaching Sociology* 7 (1979):79–86.

Lucker, Jay K. "Publishers and Librarians: Reflections of a Re-- search Library Administrator." *Library Quarterly* 54 (1984): 48–60.

McElroy, A.R. "Photocopies Versus Offprints: Does the Use of Photocopies Rather Than Offprints Affect Scholarly Communi-- cation?" *Interlending Review* 8 (1980):134--36.

Marke, Julius J. *Copyright and Intellectual Property.* New York: Fund for the Advancement of Education, 1967. ED 026 082.

Marshall, Nancy H. "Register of Copyrights' Five--year Review Report: A View From the Field." *Library Trends* 32 (1983): 165–82.

Miller, J.K. "Copyright." In Clinic on Library Applications of Data Processing, University of Illinois, 1981. Proceedings:

New Information Technologies – New Opportunities, pp. 92–100. Champaign, IL: University of Illinois, Graduate School of Library and Information Science, 1982.

Miller, J.K. "Copyright Protection For Biblographic, Numeric, Factual, and Textual Databases." *Library Trends* 32 (1983): 199–209.

"National Commission on New Technological Uses of Copyrighted Works (CONTU). Meetings One Through Seven, October 1975–June 1976." Washington, DC: Library of Congress, 1975–76. ED 127 935 through ED 127 942.

"National Commission on New Technological Uses of Copyrighted Works. Meeting Number Eight (Los Angeles, California, September 16–17, 1976). Vol. 1 and 2." Washington, DC: National Commission on New Technological Uses of Copyrighted Works, 1976. ED 135 339.

"New 'Fair Use' Defense by ARL." *Library Journal* 108 (1983); 1826.

Nitecki, D.A. "Use of an Online Circulation System for Resource Sharing." In American Society for Information Science. Conference, Anaheim, Calif., 1980. Proceedings, v. 17: *Communicating Information,* pp. 295–97. White Plains, NY: Knowledge Industry Publications for ASIS, 1980.

"No Copyright on RLIN Database." *American Libraries* 14 (1983): 511.

"OCLC Copyrighted." *College & Research Libraries News* no. 2 (1983):37.

"OCLC Copyrights Database." *Information Technology and Libraries* 2 (1983):212–13.

"OCLC Seeks Copyright Protection For Its Database." *Library Journal* 108 (1983):161–62.

Rayman, Ronald. "Automated Interlibrary Lending: An Undiagnosed Problem." *Scholarly Publishing* 12 (1980):3–11.

Richardson, E.C. "Cooperation in Lending Among College and Reference Libraries." *Collection Management* 4 (1982):49–60.

Rinzler, C.E.   "What's Fair About Fair Use?"   *Publishers Weekly* 223 (April 8, 1983):26–28.

Sharma, Ravindra N.   "Copyright – USA;   The Librarian's View." *Libri* 31 (1981):57–68.

Snyder, F.   "Copyright and the Library Reserve Room."   *Law Library Journal* 73 (1980):702–14.

Spilhaus, A.F., Jr.   "The Copyright Clearance Center."   *Scholarly Publishing* 9 (1978):143–48.

Stedman, J.C.   "Academic Library Reserves: Photocopying and the Copyright Law."   *AAUP Bulletin* 64 (1978):142–49.

Stevenson, Iris Caroline.   "Doctrine of Fair Use As It Affects Libraries."   *Law Library Journal* 68 (1975):254–73.

Thatcher, Sanford G.   "On Fair Use and Library Photocopying." *Scholarly Publishing* 9 (1978):313–34.

Trezza, A.F.   "Impact on Emerging Networks, Consortia, and the National Plan."   In *Copyright Dilemma,* pp. 179–92.   Chicago: American Library Association, 1978.

Technological Developments

Probably no other facet of librarianship has had a greater impact on attempts to ensure access to information in academic libraries as has computerization.   Online catalogs, electronic publishing, local area networks, integrated library systems, and optical disks have all had, and will continue to have, a strong effect on the ability of librarians to provide scholarly information.   In many ways, these developments have made their job easier, providing faster access to and verification of documents.   However, despite their advantages, they have presented new problems and challenges to research libraries.   Electronic publishing, for example, presents issues of access, costs, ownership, and copyright.   At the basic level, automated systems present difficulties of funding, planning, and implementation, not to mention acceptance by staff and users. In short, automation is not a quick fix to library problems and to providing access to information for scholars.   Nevertheless, it does provide some exciting opportunities and challenges which will ultimately improve access for scholars and librarians.

Aveny, Brian. "Electronic Publishing and Library Technical Services." *Library Resources & Technical Services* 28 (1984):
68–75.

Aveny, Brian. "Electronic Publishing and the Information Transfer
Process." *Special Libraries* 74 (1983):338–44.

Bezilla, Robert. "Online Messages, Files, Text, and Publishing."
Online 6 (1982):51–55.

Black, John B. "New Information Technologies: Some Observations
on What Is in Store for Libraries." Paper presented at the annual
meeting of the International Federation of Library Associations
(Manila, Philippines, August 18–23, 1980). ED 225 579.

Blair, John C., Jr. "Systems Suitable for Information Professionals."
Online 7 (1983):36–43,46–48.

Brownrigg, Edwin et al. "Technical Services in the Age of Electronic
Publishing." *Library Resources & Technical Services* 28 (1984):
59–67.

Bullard, David. "Local Area Networks." *CAUSE/EFFECT* 6,
no. 6 (Nov. 1983):12–15.

Butler, Meredith. "Electronic Publishing and Its Impact on Libraries: A Literature Review." *Library Resources & Technical
Services* 28 (1984):41–51,54–58.

Chadwyck–Healey, Charles. "The Future of Microform in an Electronic Age." *Wilson Library Bulletin* 58 (1983):270–73.

Cotton, Ira W., ed. "Computer Science & Technology: Local
Area Networking." Washington, DC: National Bureau of Stan-
dards, Institute for Computer Sciences and Technology, 1978.
NBS–SP–500–31. ED 167 172.

de Gennaro, Richard. "Library Automation: Changing Patterns
and New Directions." *Library Journal* 101 (1976):175–83.

"Effects of New Technologies." *Social and Labour Bulletin* 3
(1980):273–82.

Farr, Rick C. "The Local Area Network (LAN) and Library Automation." *Library Journal* 108 (1983):2130–32.

Featheringham, T.R. "Paperless Publishing and Potential Institutional Change." *Scholarly Publishing* 13 (1981):19–30.

Fussler, Herman H. *Research Libraries and Technology; A Report to the Sloan Foundation.* Chicago: University of Chicago Press, 1973.

Galloway, Emily, and Paris, Judith. "Information Providers and Videodisc/Optical Disk Technology." *Journal of the American Society for Information Science* 34 (1983):414–16.

Goldstein, Charles M. "Optical Disk Technology and Information." *Science* 215 (1982):862–68.

Graham, Peter S. "Technology and the Online Catalog." *Library Resources & Technical Services* 27 (1983):18–35.

"International Congress on Universal Availability of Publications (Paris, France, May 3–7, 1982). Main Working Document. Including Annotated Programme and Summary." The Hague (Netherlands): IFLA; Paris: UNESCO, 1982. ED 226 761.

King, Donald W. "Electronic Publishing and Its Implications for Libraries." 1979. ED 196 435.

Koch, H. William. "Impact of Electronic Publishing on Scholarly Journals." Paper presented at a Joint Conference of the Society of Scholarly Publishing, the Council of Biology Editions, and the International Federation of Scientific Editors (May 15–20, 1983). ED 235 789.

Lancaster, F.W. *Libraries and Librarians in an Age of Electronics.* Arlington, VA: Information Resources Press, 1982.

Lancaster, F.W., and Neway, Julie M. "The Future of Indexing and Abstracting Services." *Journal of the American Society for Information Science* 33 (1982):183–89.

Lunin, Lois F., and Paris, Judith, eds. "Perspectives on Videodisc and Optical Disk: Technology, Research, and Applications." Special issue of *Journal of the American Society for Information Science* 34 (1983):405–440. Contains six articles.

McGraw, Harold W., Jr. "Responding to Information Needs in the 1980s." *Wilson Library Bulletin* 54 (1979):160–64.

Matthews, Joseph R.   "20 Qs and As on Automated Integrated Library Systems." *American Libraries* 13 (1982):367–71.

Mebane, Donna Davis, ed. *Solving College and University Problems Through Technology.* Princeton, NJ: Interuniversity Communications Council (EDUCOM), 1981.   Papers presented at the EDUCOM Annual Conference, Atlanta, Georgia, October 1–3, 1980. ED 220 095.

Neavill, Gordon B.   "Electronic Publishing, Libraries, and the Survival of Information." *Library Resources & Technical Services* 28 (1984):76–89.

"Person to Person Networks: Human Communication and Information Exchange Via Computer." *ASIS Bulletin* 4 (1978):9–23.

Siegel, E., Schubin, M., and Merrill, P.F.   *Videodiscs: The Technology, the Applications, and the Future.*   White Plains, NY: Knowledge Industry Publications, 1980.

Stirling, John F.   "Technological Developments in Information Transfer: Some Implications for Academic Libraries." *Journal of Librarianship* 14 (1982):235–46.

Turock, B.J.   "Technology and the Post–industrial Society: The Academic Library in the 1980s and Beyond." *Catholic Library World* 55 (1984):298–304.

Turoff, Murray, and Hiltz, Starr Roxanne.   "The Electronic Journal: A Progress Report." *Journal of the American Society for Information Science* 33 (1982):195–202.

Veaner, Allen B.   "Librarians: The Next Generation." *Library Journal* 109 (1984):623–25.

Williams, M.E.   "Impact of Machine–readable Data Bases on Library and Information Services." *Information Processing and Management* 13 (1977):95–107.

Wolfe, Mary Grantham.   "The Future of the Library in an Electronic Society: The State of the Art." 1980. ED 203 883.